Max Axiom and the Society of Super Scientists

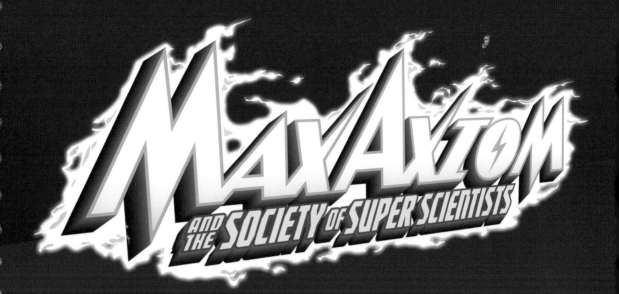

Polar Ice Meltdown

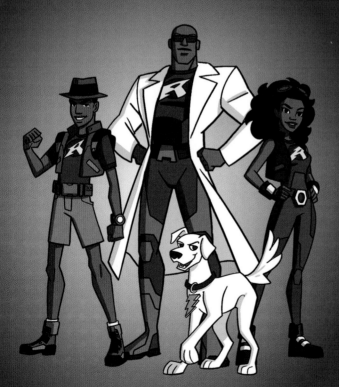

Written by Carol Kim
Illustrated by Erik Doescher

CAPSTONE PRESS
a capstone imprint

Published by Capstone Press, an imprint of Capstone.
1710 Roe Crest Drive
North Mankato, Minnesota 56003
capstonepub.com

Library of Congress Cataloging-in-Publication Data
Names: Kim, Carol, author. | Doescher, Erik, illustrator.
Title: Polar ice meltdown : a Max Axiom super scientist adventure / Carol Kim ; illustrated by Erik Doescher.
Description: North Mankato, Minnesota : Capstone Press, [2022] | Series: Max Axiom and the society of super scientists | Includes bibliographical references and index. | Audience: Ages 8–11 | Audience: Grades 4–6
Identifiers: LCCN 2021012699 (print) | LCCN 2021012700 (ebook) | ISBN 9781663921734 (paperback) | ISBN 9781663907479 (hardcover) | ISBN 9781663907448 (ebook PDF) | ISBN 9781663907462 (kindle edition)
Subjects: LCSH: Climatic changes—Polar regions—Juvenile literature. | Climatic changes—Polar regions—Comic books, strips, etc. | Global warming—Polar regions—Juvenile literature. | Glaciers—Climatic factors—Polar regions—Juvenile literature. | Ice—Antarctica—Juvenile literature. | Ice—Arctic regions—Juvenile literature.
Classification: LCC QC903.15 .K54 2022 (print) | LCC QC903.15 (ebook) | DDC 363.738/74—dc23
LC record available at https://lccn.loc.gov/2021012699
LC ebook record available at https://lccn.loc.gov/2021012700

Summary: Earth's polar ice is disappearing! But why are ice caps, glaciers, and icebergs melting, and how does it impact the planet? In this nonfiction graphic novel, Max Axiom and the Society of Super Scientists are on a mission to find out.

Editorial Credits
Editors: Abby Huff and Aaron Sautter; Designer: Brann Garvey; Media Researcher: Svetlana Zhurkin; Production Specialist: Kathy McColley

All internet sites appearing in back matter were available and accurate when this book was sent to press.

Printed and bound in the United States of America. PO4270

TABLE OF CONTENTS

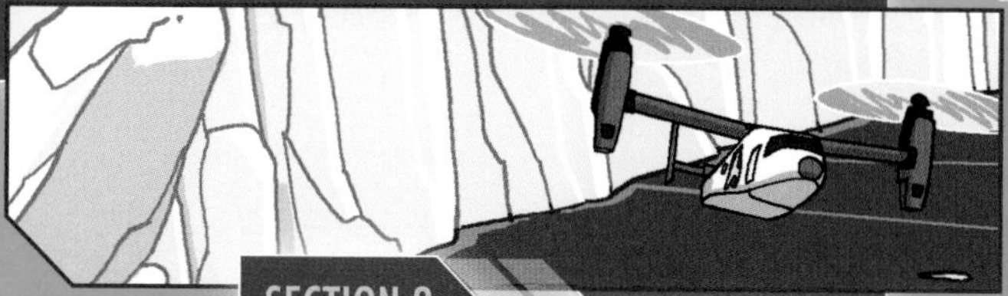

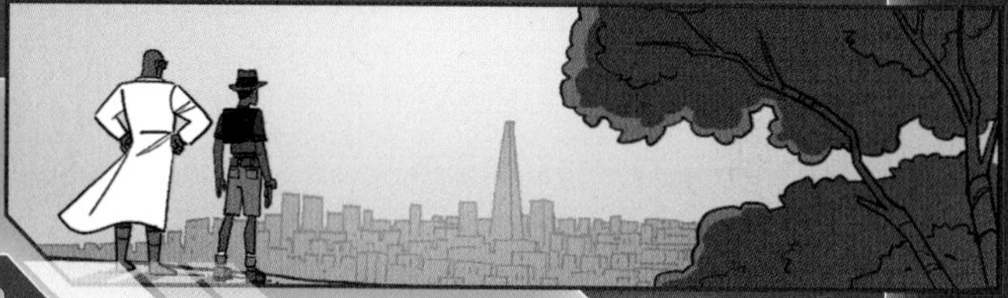

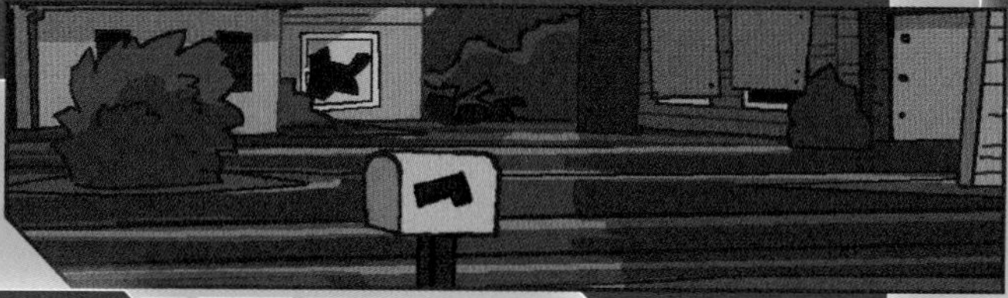

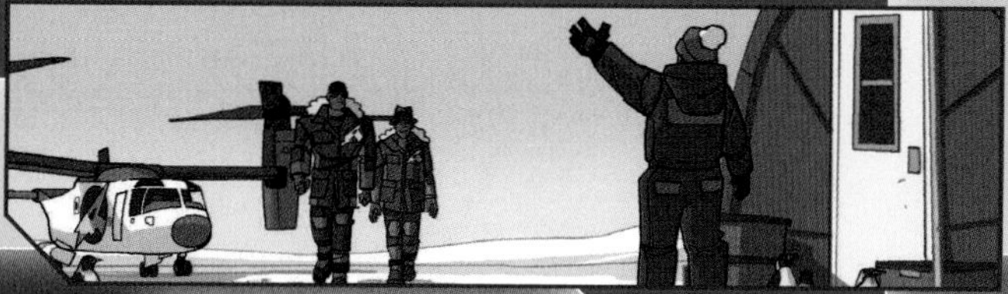

THE SOCIETY OF SUPER SCIENTISTS

MAX AXIOM

After years of study, Max Axiom, the world's first Super Scientist, knew the mysteries of the universe were too vast for one person alone to uncover. So Max created the Society of Super Scientists! Using their superpowers and super-smarts, this talented group investigates today's most urgent scientific and environmental issues and learns about actions everyone can take to solve them.

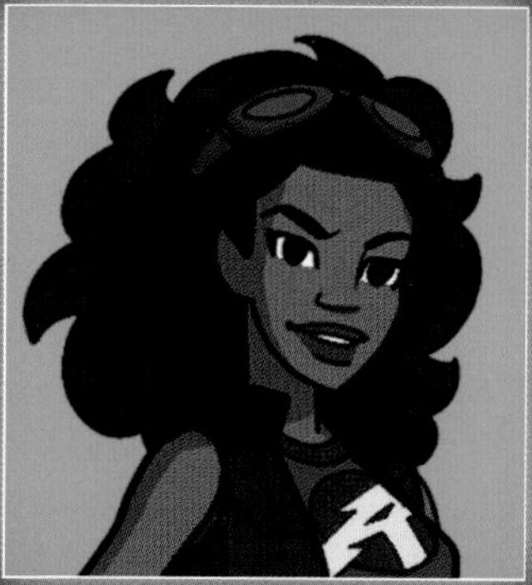

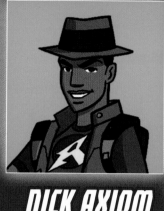

LIZZY AXIOM

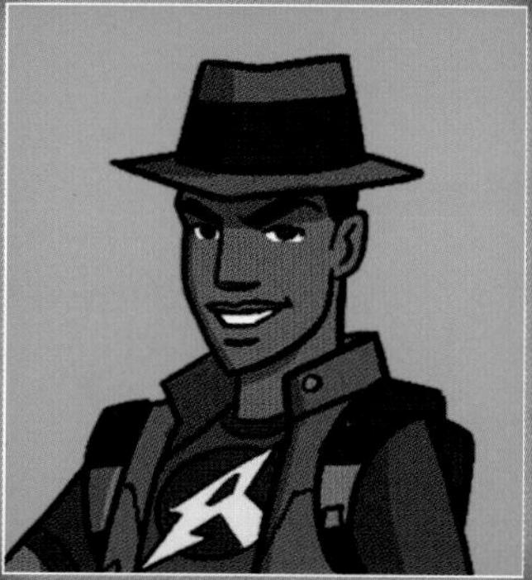

NICK AXIOM

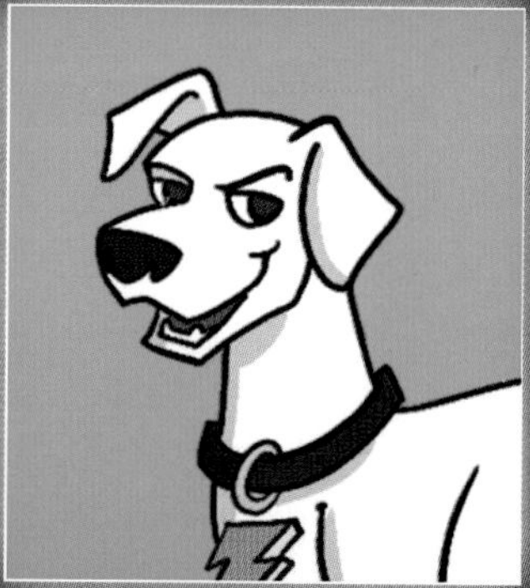

SPARK

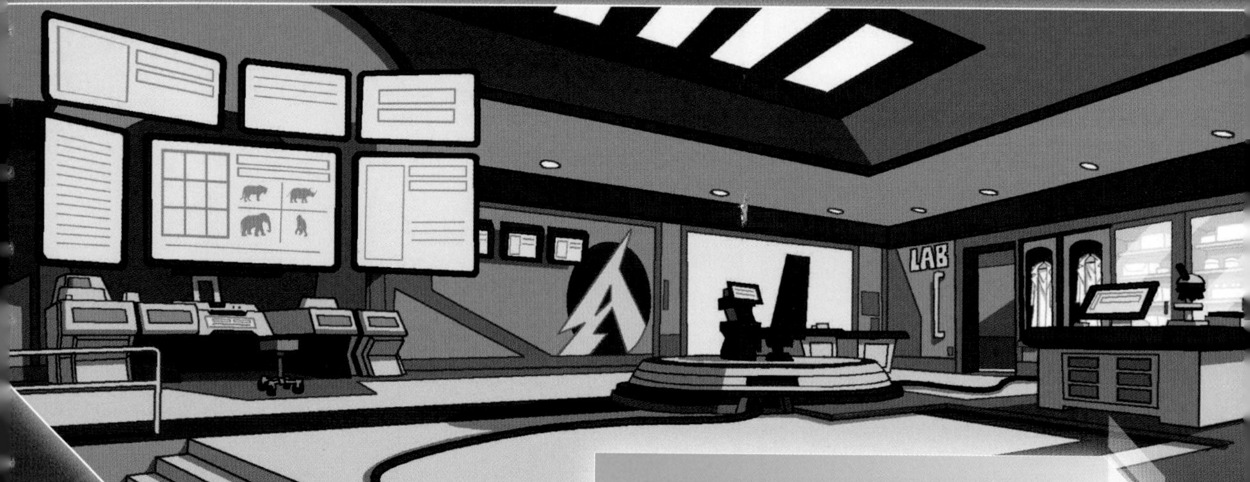
LAB

THE DISCOVERY LAB

Home of the Society of Super Scientists, this state-of-the-art lab houses advanced tools for cutting-edge research and radical scientific innovation. More importantly, it is a space for Super Scientists to collaborate and share knowledge as they work together to tackle any challenge.

SECTION 1: *DISAPPEARING POLAR ICE*

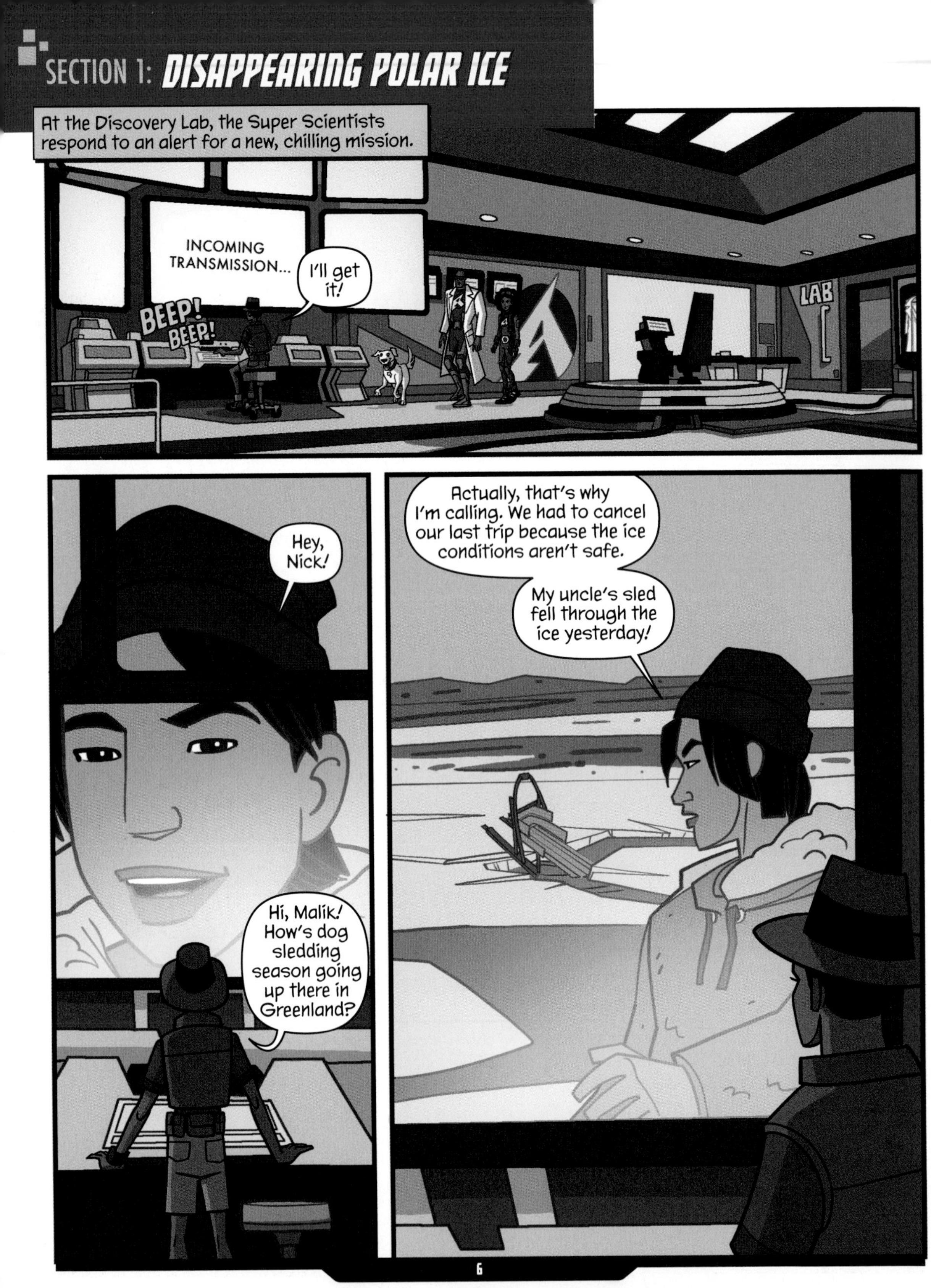
At the Discovery Lab, the Super Scientists respond to an alert for a new, chilling mission.
INCOMING TRANSMISSION...
I'll get it!
BEEP! BEEP!
LAB
Hey, Nick!
Hi, Malik! How's dog sledding season going up there in Greenland?
Actually, that's why I'm calling. We had to cancel our last trip because the ice conditions aren't safe.
My uncle's sled fell through the ice yesterday!

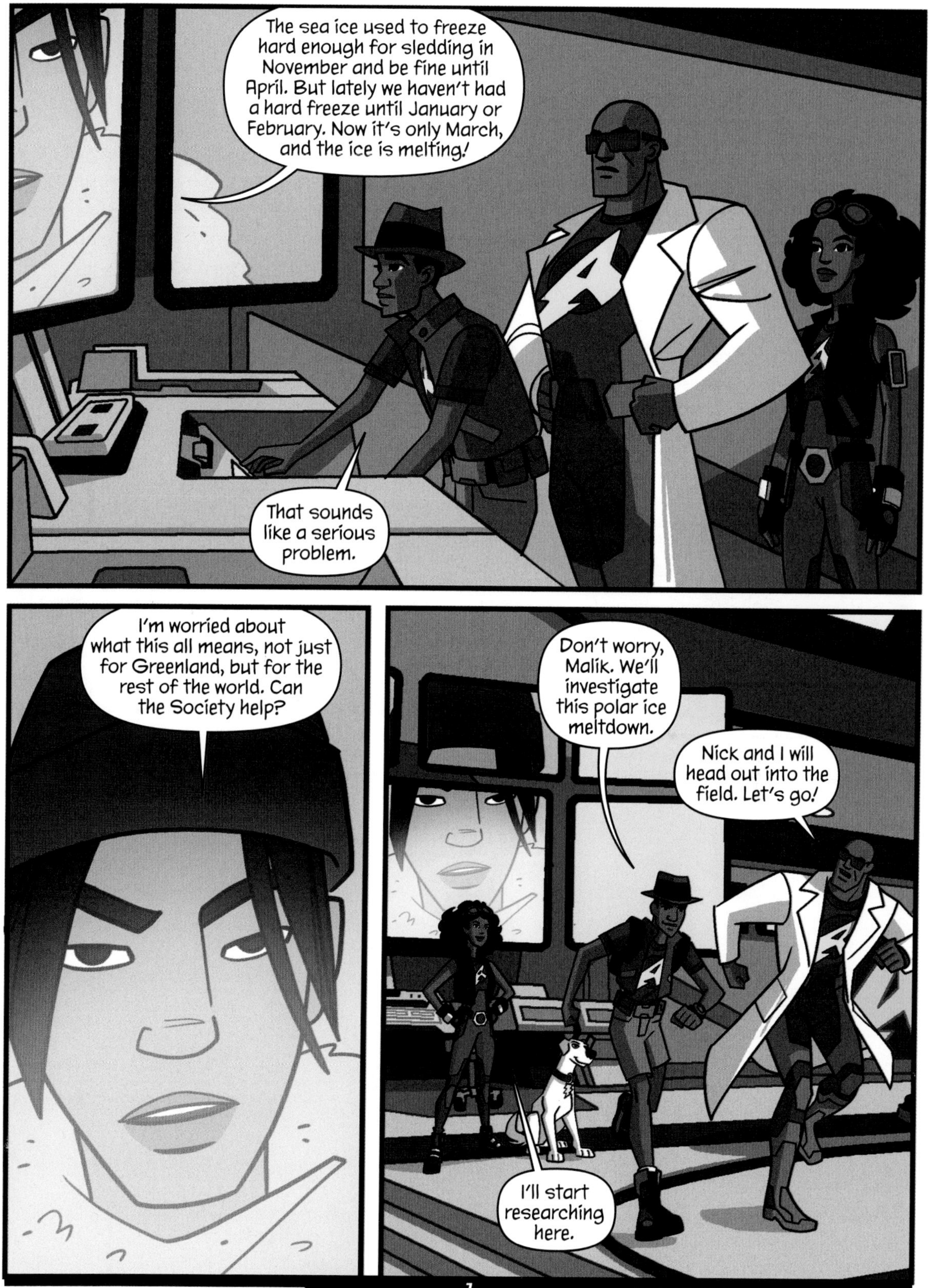
The sea ice used to freeze hard enough for sledding in November and be fine until April. But lately we haven't had a hard freeze until January or February. Now it's only March, and the ice is melting!
That sounds like a serious problem.
I'm worried about what this all means, not just for Greenland, but for the rest of the world. Can the Society help?
Don't worry, Malik. We'll investigate this polar ice meltdown.
Nick and I will head out into the field. Let's go!
I'll start researching here.

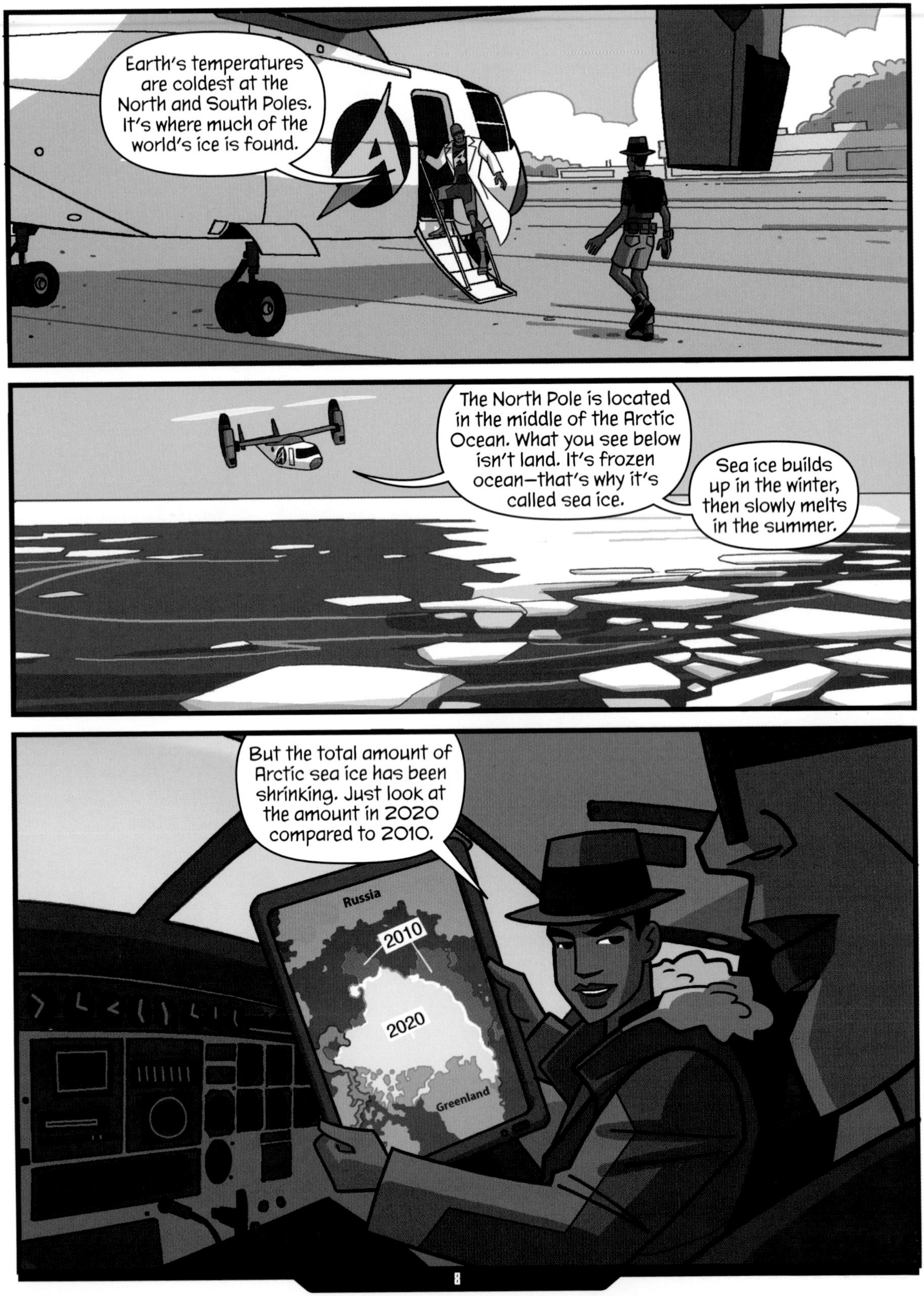
Earth's temperatures are coldest at the North and South Poles. It's where much of the world's ice is found.
The North Pole is located in the middle of the Arctic Ocean. What you see below isn't land. It's frozen ocean—that's why it's called sea ice.
Sea ice builds up in the winter, then slowly melts in the summer.
But the total amount of Arctic sea ice has been shrinking. Just look at the amount in 2020 compared to 2010.
Russia
2010
2020
Greenland

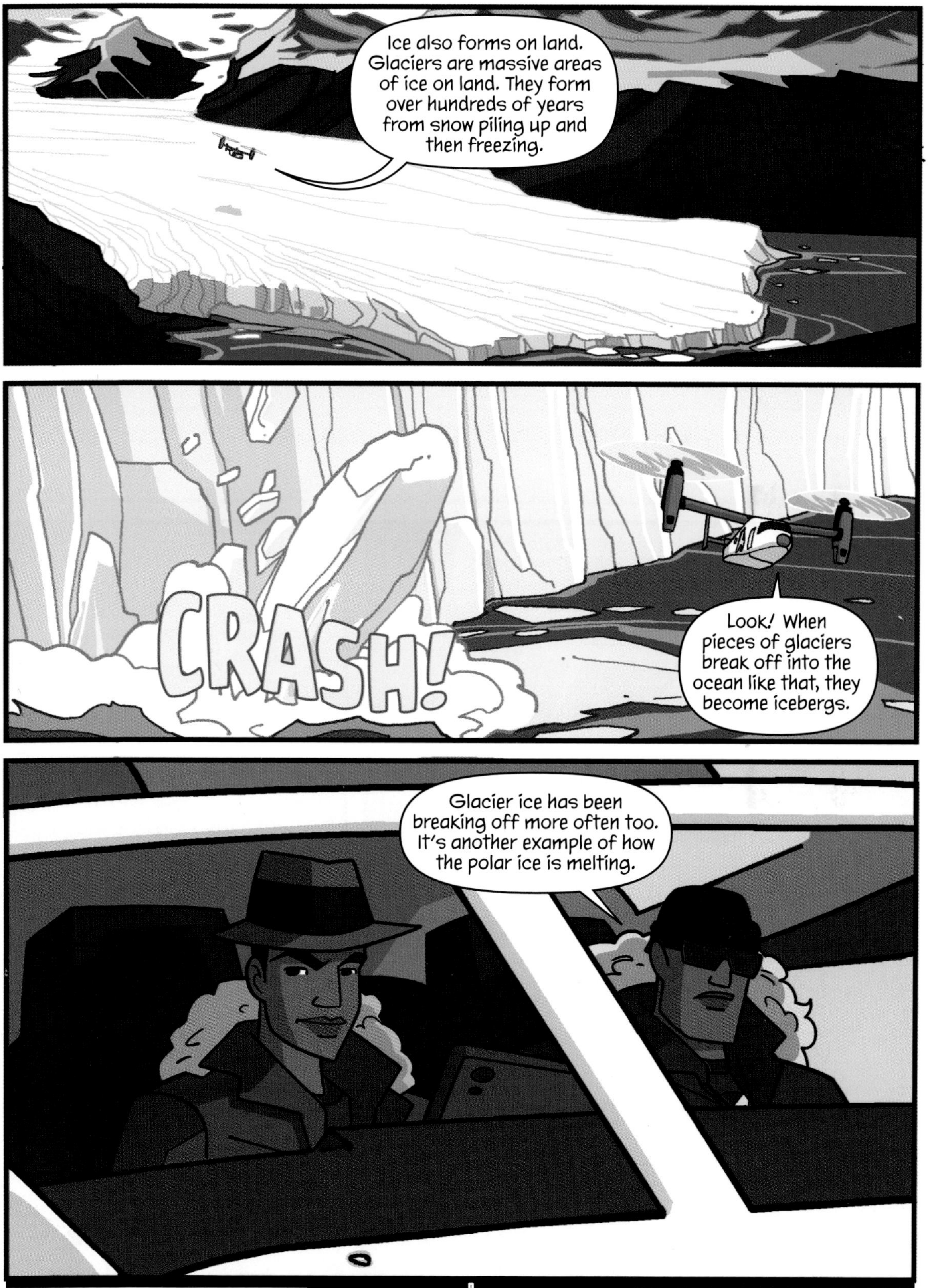
Ice also forms on land. Glaciers are massive areas of ice on land. They form over hundreds of years from snow piling up and then freezing.
CRASH!
Look! When pieces of glaciers break off into the ocean like that, they become icebergs.
Glacier ice has been breaking off more often too. It's another example of how the polar ice is melting.

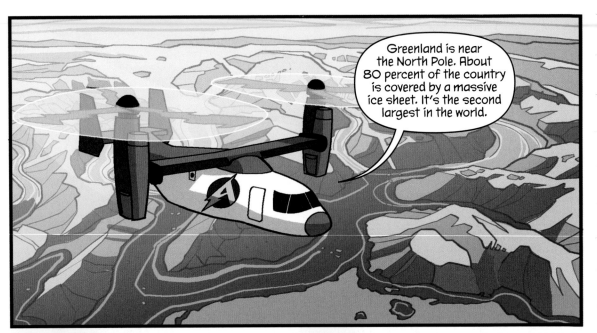

Greenland is near the North Pole. About 80 percent of the country is covered by a massive ice sheet. It's the second largest in the world.

This land ice is melting too. Since 2002, the Greenland ice sheet has been losing about 269 billion tons of ice per year. But what's happening at the South Pole?

Let's zip down there to check it out.

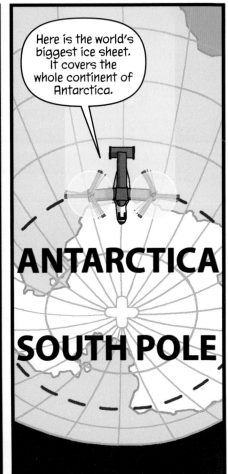

Here is the world's biggest ice sheet. It covers the whole continent of Antarctica.

ANTARCTICA

SOUTH POLE

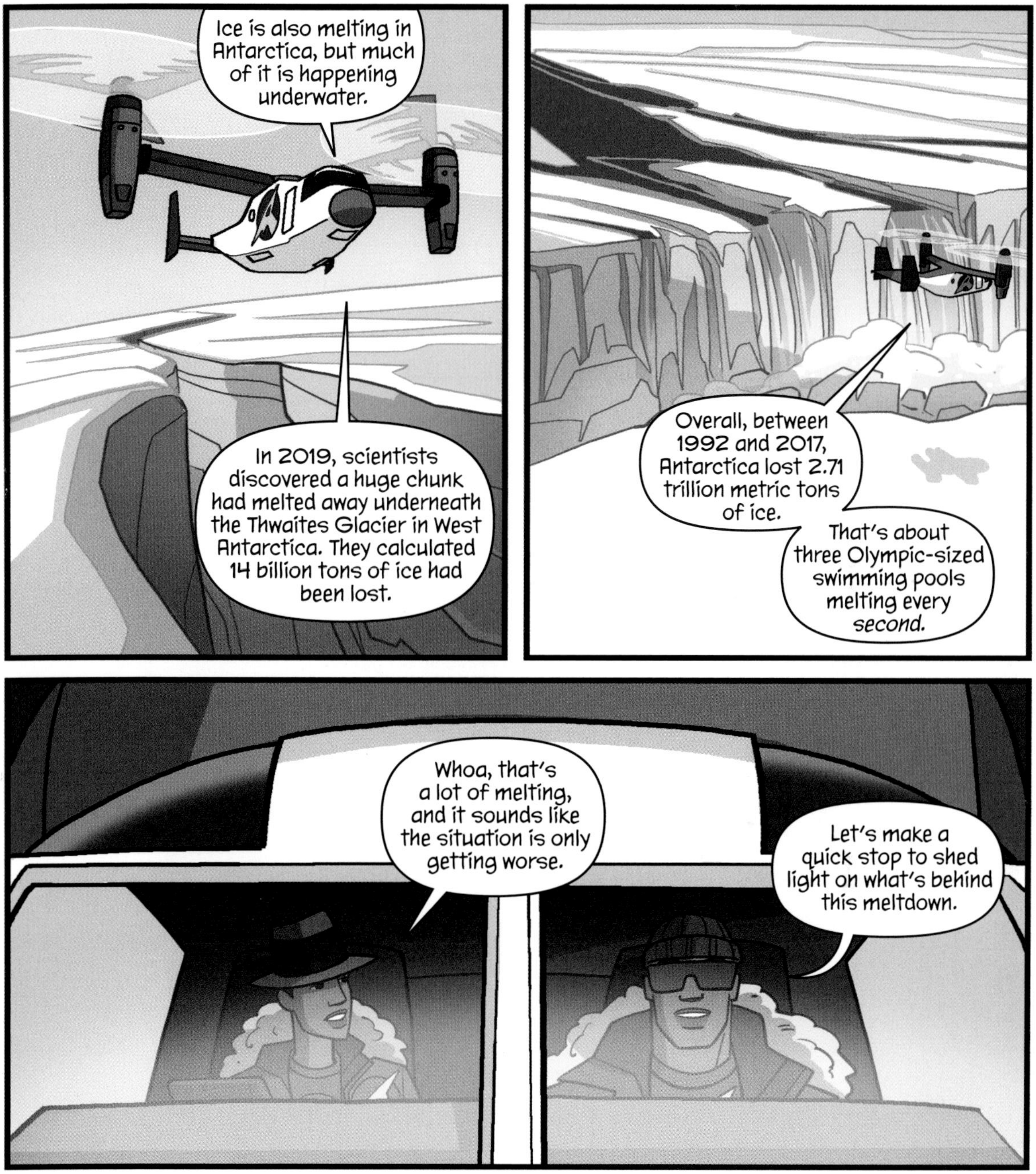
Ice is also melting in Antarctica, but much of it is happening underwater.
In 2019, scientists discovered a huge chunk had melted away underneath the Thwaites Glacier in West Antarctica. They calculated 14 billion tons of ice had been lost.
Overall, between 1992 and 2017, Antarctica lost 2.71 trillion metric tons of ice.
That's about three Olympic-sized swimming pools melting every *second.*
Whoa, that's a lot of melting, and it sounds like the situation is only getting worse.
Let's make a quick stop to shed light on what's behind this meltdown.

FROZEN FRESHWATER

Most of the freshwater on Earth, about 70 percent, is frozen into ice on the North and South Poles. This amounts to 7.2 million cubic miles (30 million cubic kilometers) of ice. It's so much ice that if all of it were spread out in a layer 1 mile (1.6 km) thick, it would completely cover North America.

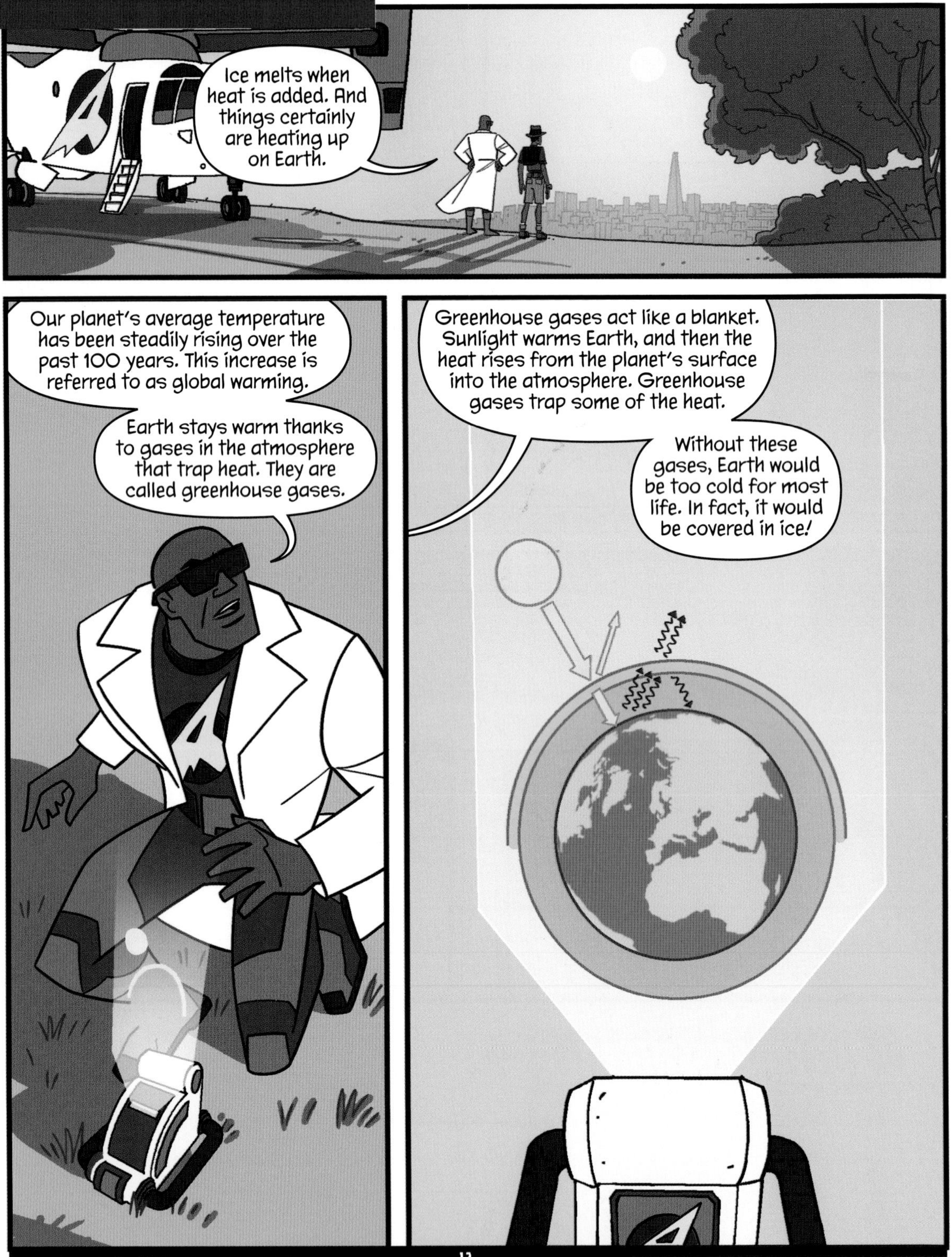
Ice melts when heat is added. And things certainly are heating up on Earth.
Our planet's average temperature has been steadily rising over the past 100 years. This increase is referred to as global warming.
Earth stays warm thanks to gases in the atmosphere that trap heat. They are called greenhouse gases.
Greenhouse gases act like a blanket. Sunlight warms Earth, and then the heat rises from the planet's surface into the atmosphere. Greenhouse gases trap some of the heat.
Without these gases, Earth would be too cold for most life. In fact, it would be covered in ice!

But human activities are putting more greenhouse gases into the air.

One major greenhouse gas is carbon dioxide. It's produced by burning fossil fuels, such as coal, oil, and natural gas. Cars, factories, and power plants all burn fossil fuels.

As more greenhouse gases collect in the atmosphere, more heat is trapped, and Earth's temperature rises.

In fact, the average global temperature has risen about 1.8 degrees Fahrenheit, or 0.98 degrees Celsius, over the past 100 years.

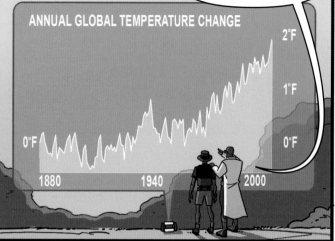

ANNUAL GLOBAL TEMPERATURE CHANGE

2°F

1°F

0°F

1880   1940   2000

A small change in average temperatures can have a big effect on climate. Just a one degree increase can cause more extreme weather, such as droughts, floods, and hurricanes.

And the melting of polar ice.

What's worse, the effects of global warming are stronger in the Arctic. Air temperatures here are rising at twice the global average rate.
Arctic ice helps cool Earth. The white ice and snow reflect a lot of sunlight back into space. This reflection is called the "albedo effect."
90%
10%
6%
94%
The same effect explains why wearing a white shirt in summer helps keep you cooler than a dark one. A dark shirt absorbs more of the sun's energy.
But as global temperatures rise, more ice melts. There is not as much white surface to reflect the sun's rays.
And because the ice-free land and ocean is darker, more energy is absorbed. Even more ice melts. The cycle of warming repeats itself.

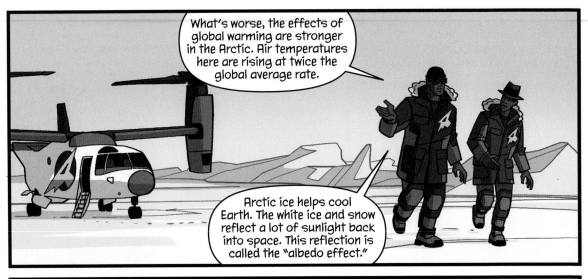

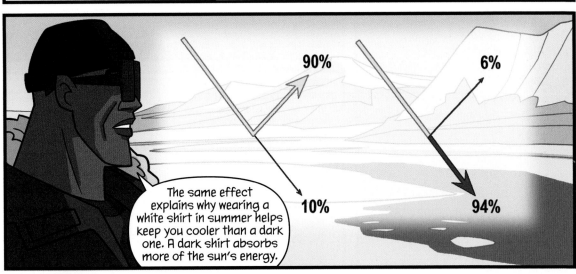

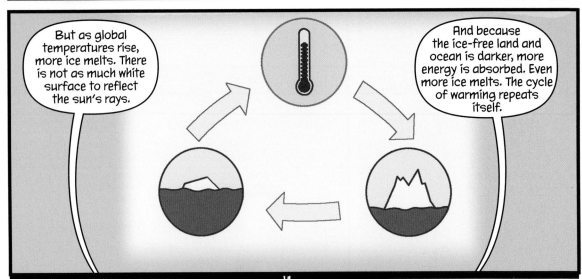

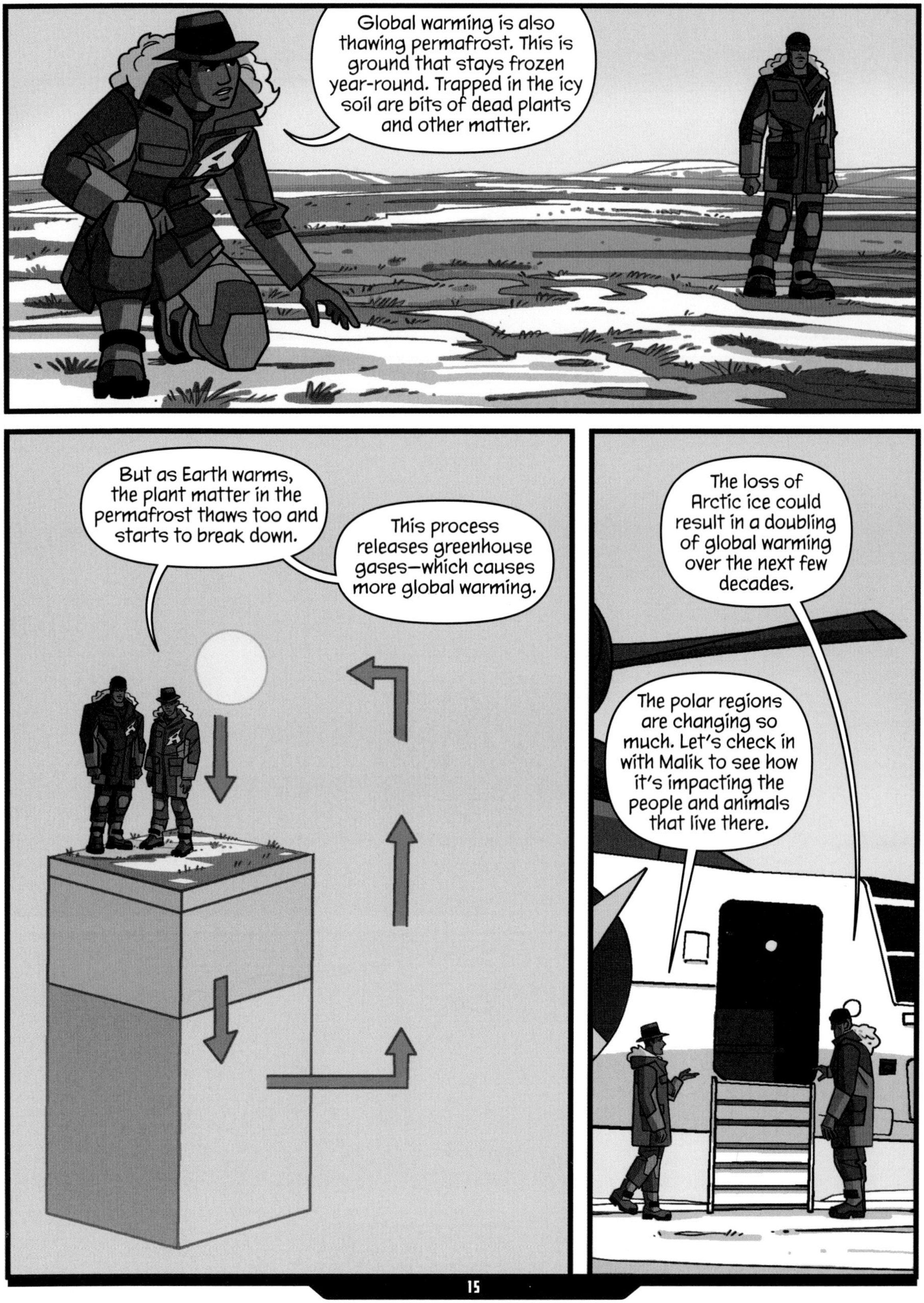

Global warming is also thawing permafrost. This is ground that stays frozen year-round. Trapped in the icy soil are bits of dead plants and other matter.
But as Earth warms, the plant matter in the permafrost thaws too and starts to break down.
This process releases greenhouse gases—which causes more global warming.
The loss of Arctic ice could result in a doubling of global warming over the next few decades.
The polar regions are changing so much. Let's check in with Malik to see how it's impacting the people and animals that live there.

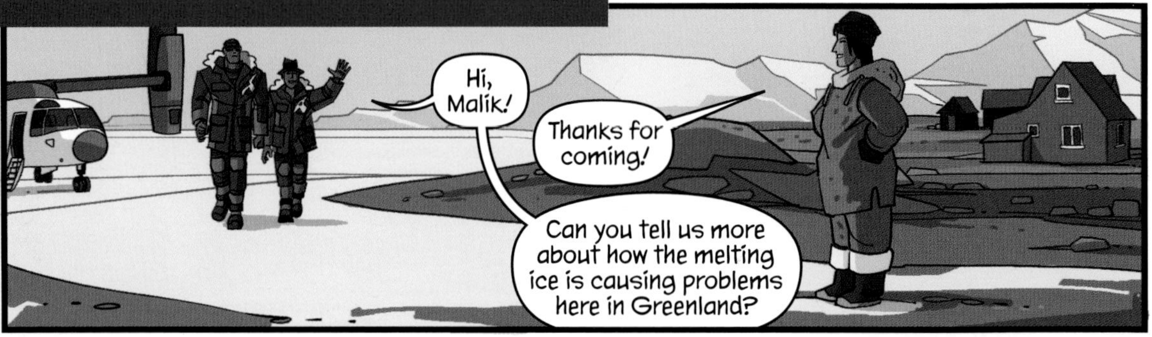
Hi, Malik!
Thanks for coming!
Can you tell us more about how the melting ice is causing problems here in Greenland?

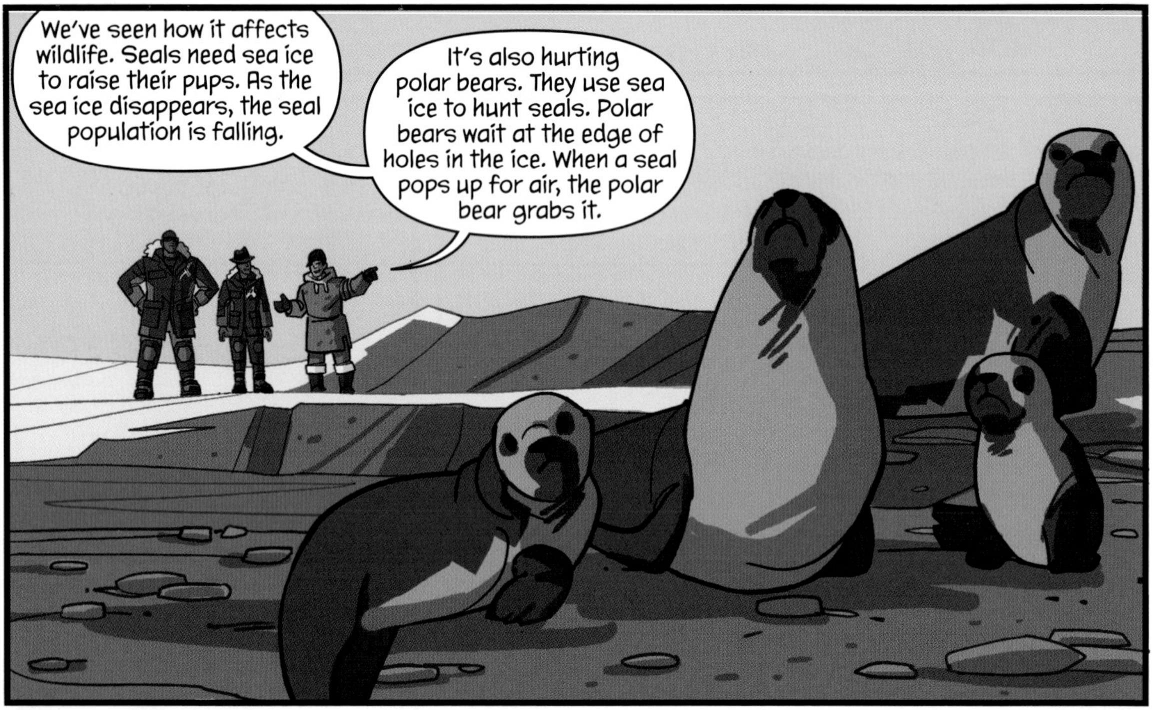
We've seen how it affects wildlife. Seals need sea ice to raise their pups. As the sea ice disappears, the seal population is falling.
It's also hurting polar bears. They use sea ice to hunt seals. Polar bears wait at the edge of holes in the ice. When a seal pops up for air, the polar bear grabs it.

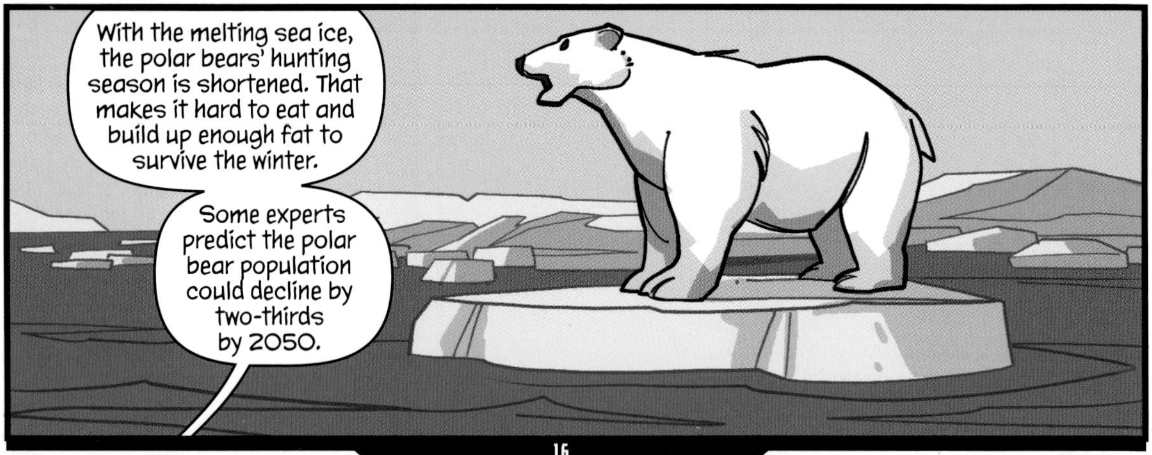
With the melting sea ice, the polar bears' hunting season is shortened. That makes it hard to eat and build up enough fat to survive the winter.
Some experts predict the polar bear population could decline by two-thirds by 2050.

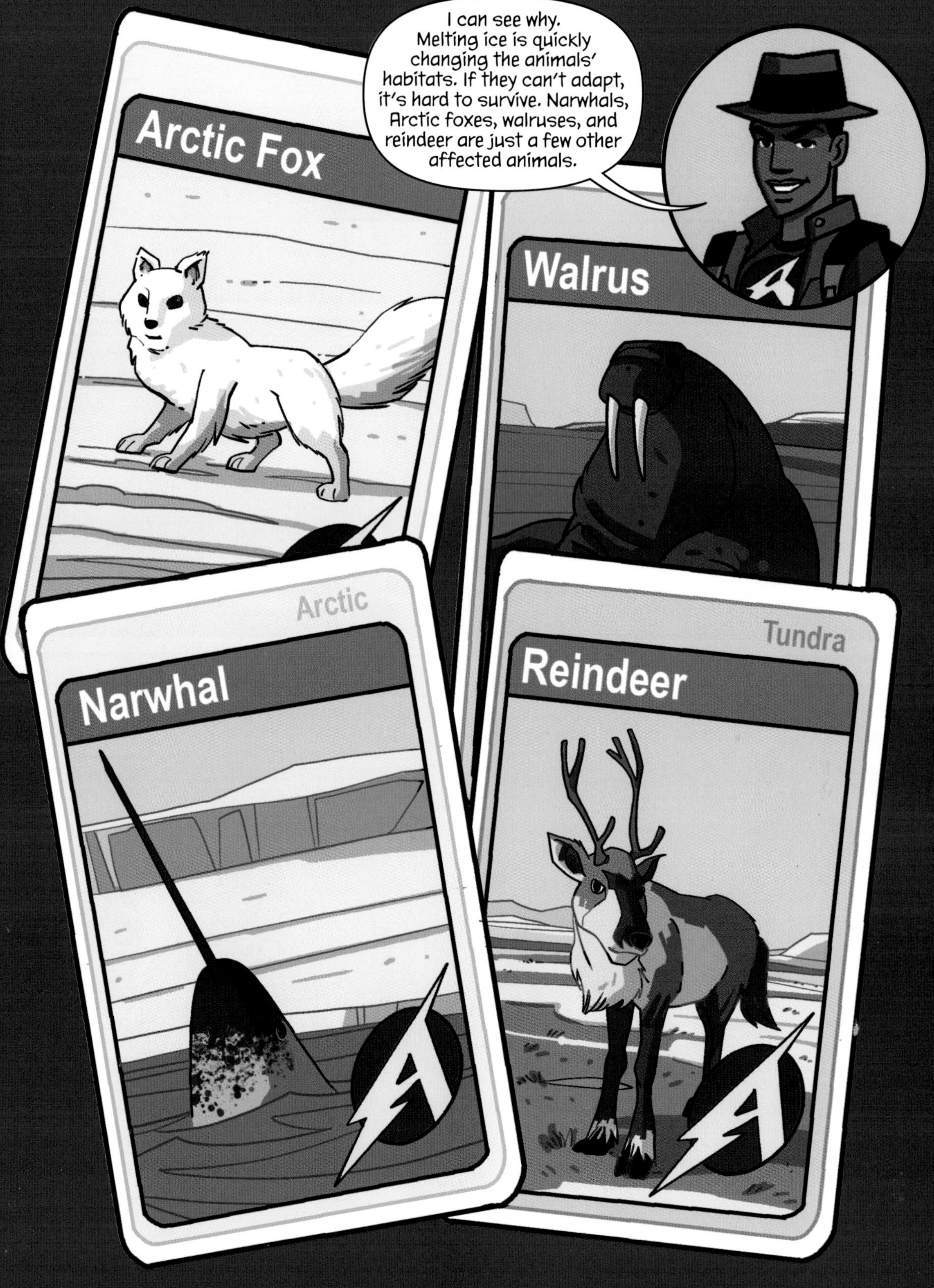
I can see why. Melting ice is quickly changing the animals' habitats. If they can't adapt, it's hard to survive. Narwhals, Arctic foxes, walruses, and reindeer are just a few other affected animals.
Arctic Fox
Walrus
Arctic
Narwhal
Tundra
Reindeer

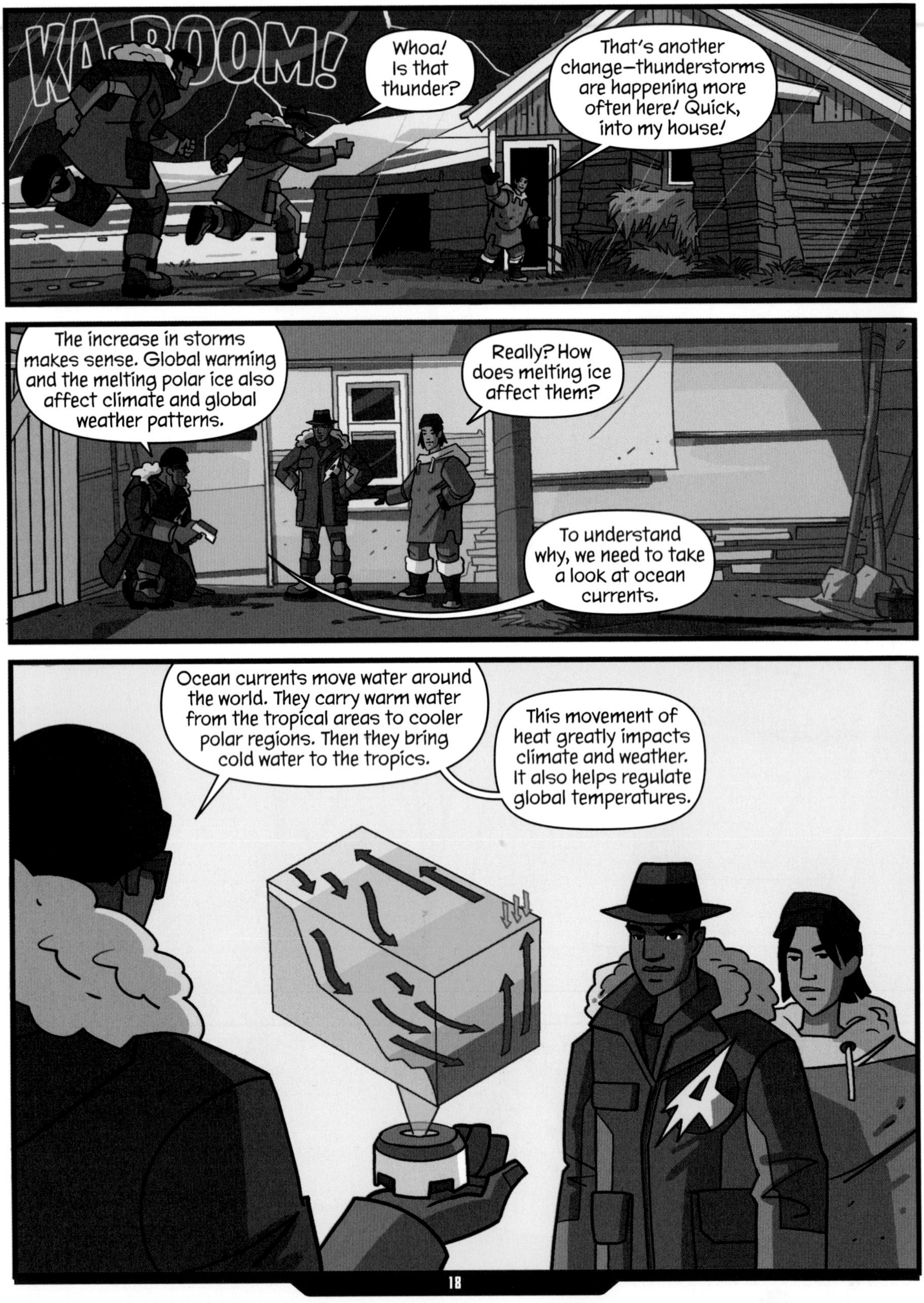
KA-BOOM!
Whoa! Is that thunder?
That's another change—thunderstorms are happening more often here! Quick, into my house!
The increase in storms makes sense. Global warming and the melting polar ice also affect climate and global weather patterns.
Really? How does melting ice affect them?
To understand why, we need to take a look at ocean currents.
Ocean currents move water around the world. They carry warm water from the tropical areas to cooler polar regions. Then they bring cold water to the tropics.
This movement of heat greatly impacts climate and weather. It also helps regulate global temperatures.

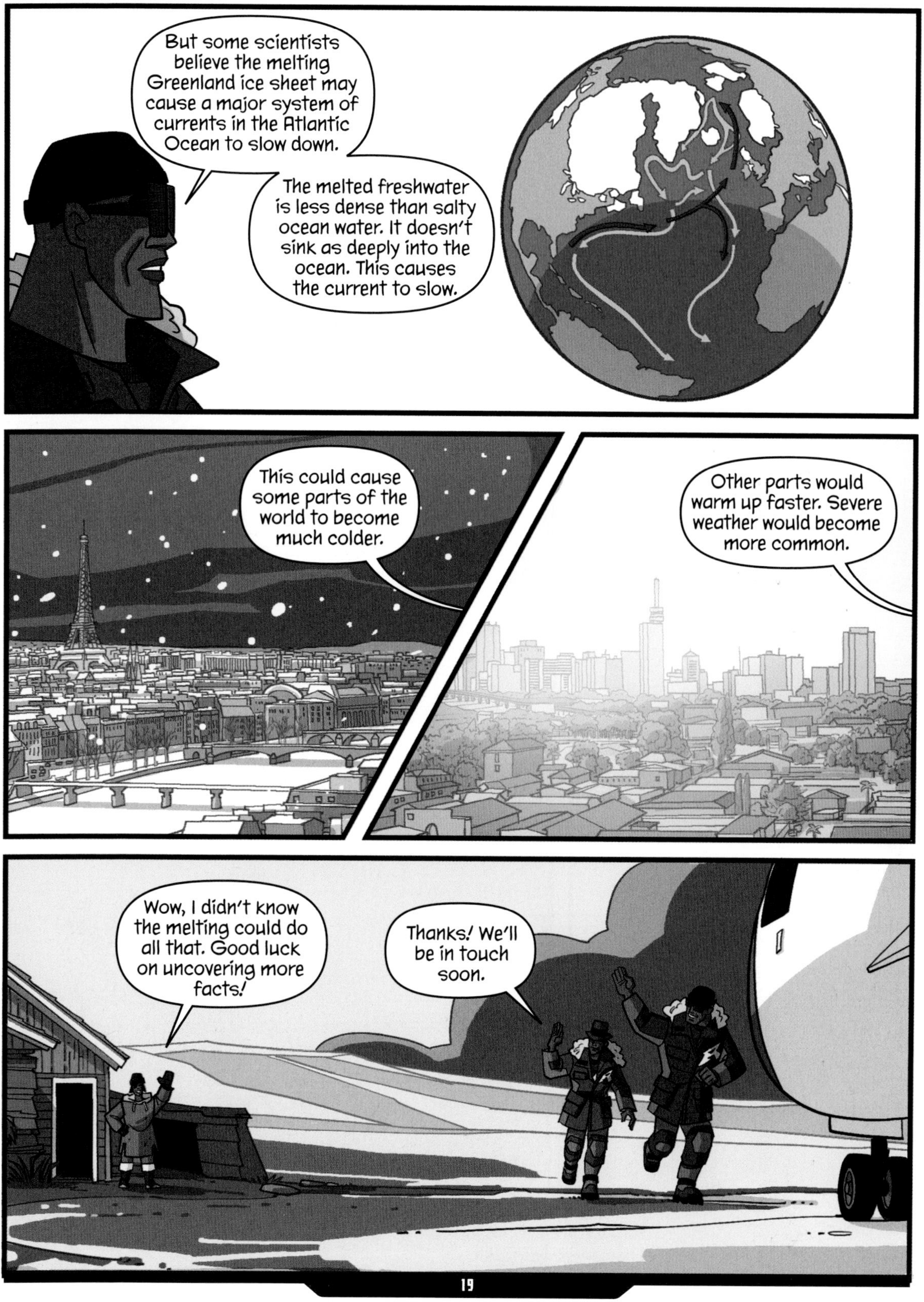

But some scientists believe the melting Greenland ice sheet may cause a major system of currents in the Atlantic Ocean to slow down.
The melted freshwater is less dense than salty ocean water. It doesn't sink as deeply into the ocean. This causes the current to slow.
This could cause some parts of the world to become much colder.
Other parts would warm up faster. Severe weather would become more common.
Wow, I didn't know the melting could do all that. Good luck on uncovering more facts!
Thanks! We'll be in touch soon.

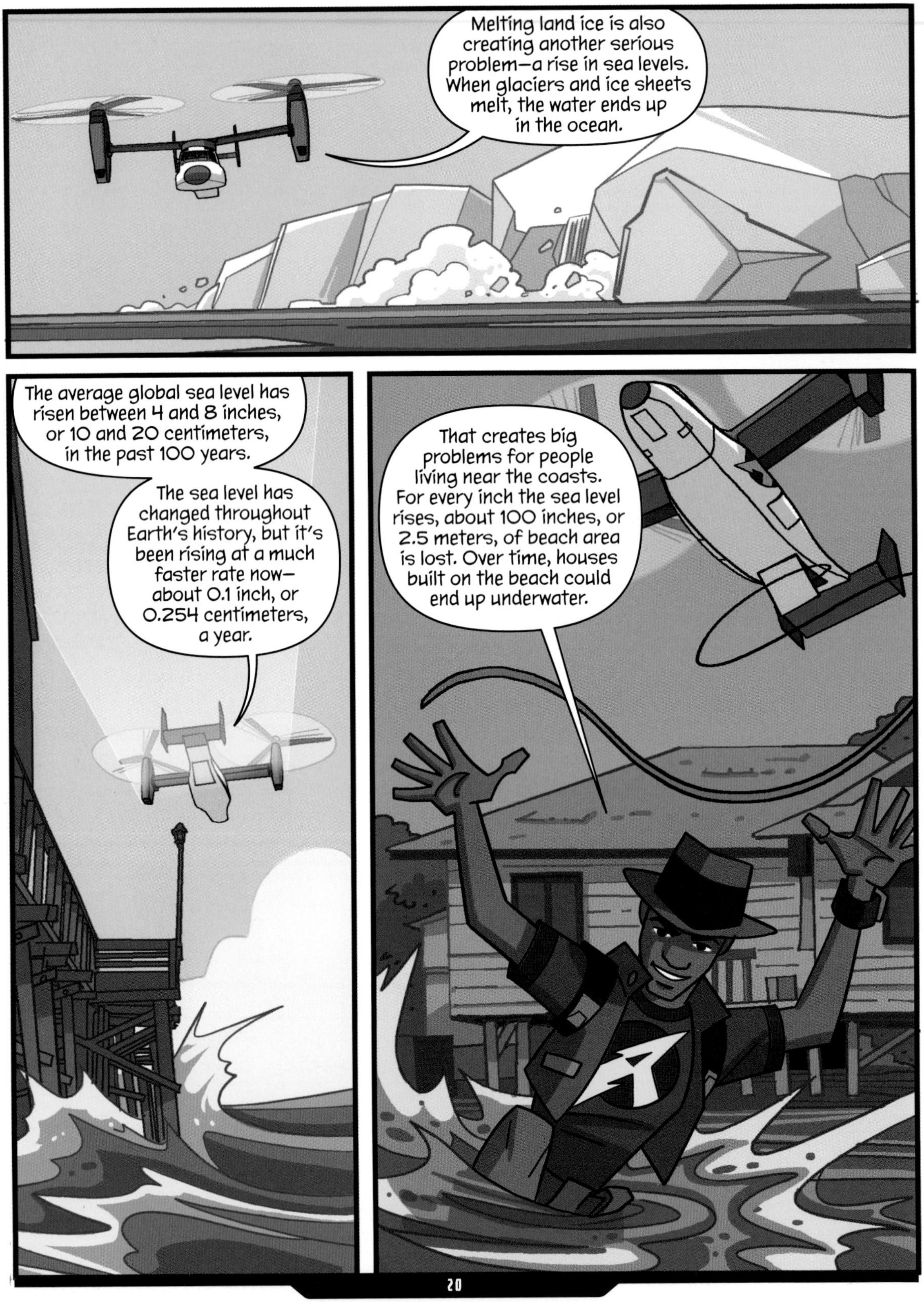
Melting land ice is also creating another serious problem—a rise in sea levels. When glaciers and ice sheets melt, the water ends up in the ocean.
The average global sea level has risen between 4 and 8 inches, or 10 and 20 centimeters, in the past 100 years.
The sea level has changed throughout Earth's history, but it's been rising at a much faster rate now—about 0.1 inch, or 0.254 centimeters, a year.
That creates big problems for people living near the coasts. For every inch the sea level rises, about 100 inches, or 2.5 meters, of beach area is lost. Over time, houses built on the beach could end up underwater.

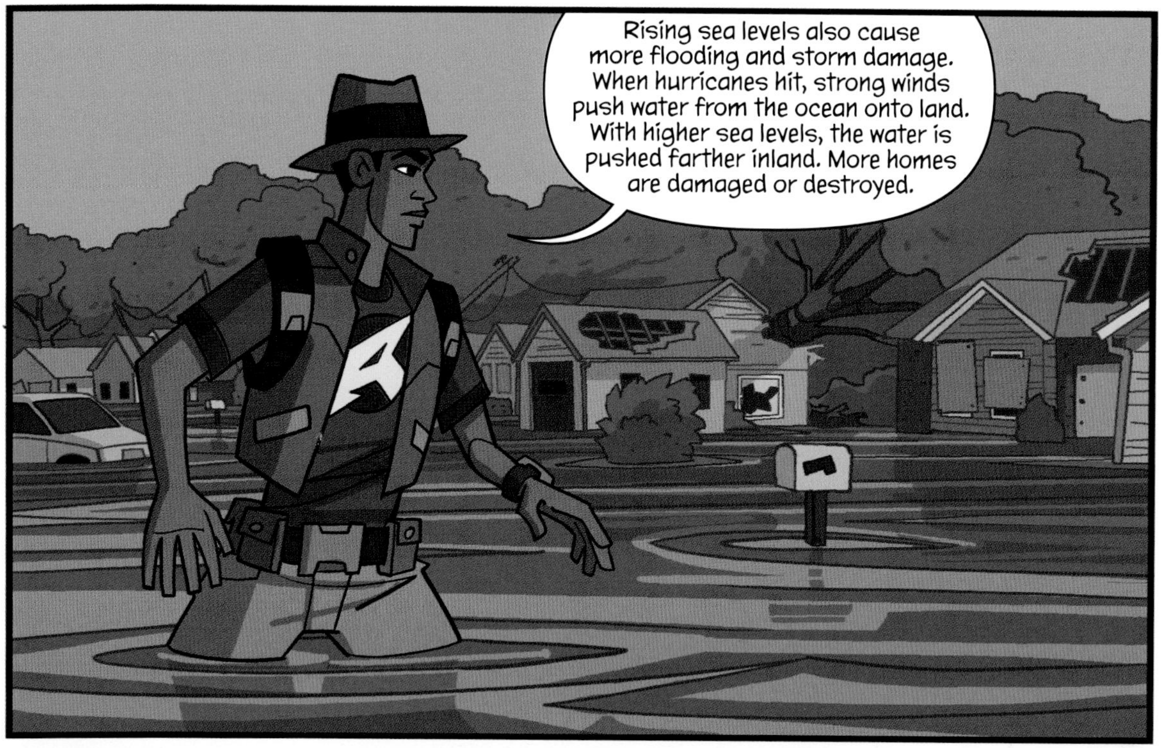
Rising sea levels also cause more flooding and storm damage. When hurricanes hit, strong winds push water from the ocean onto land. With higher sea levels, the water is pushed farther inland. More homes are damaged or destroyed.

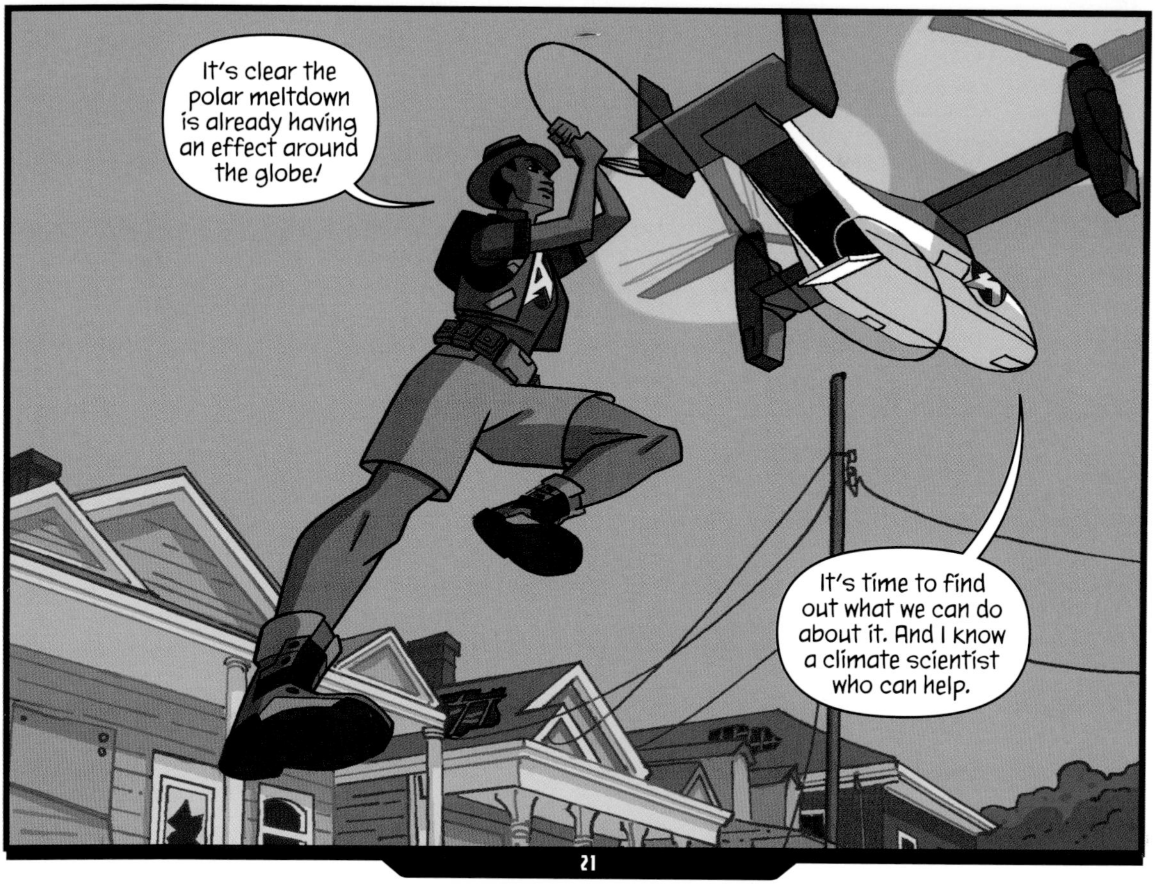
It's clear the polar meltdown is already having an effect around the globe!
It's time to find out what we can do about it. And I know a climate scientist who can help.

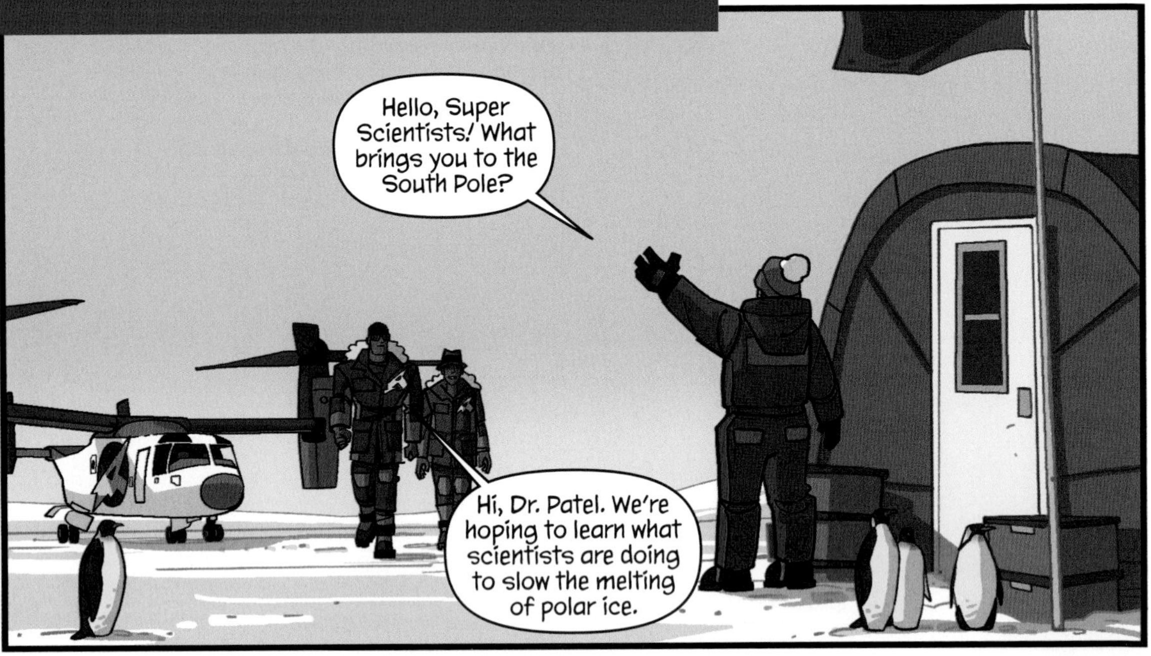
Hello, Super Scientists! What brings you to the South Pole?
Hi, Dr. Patel. We're hoping to learn what scientists are doing to slow the melting of polar ice.

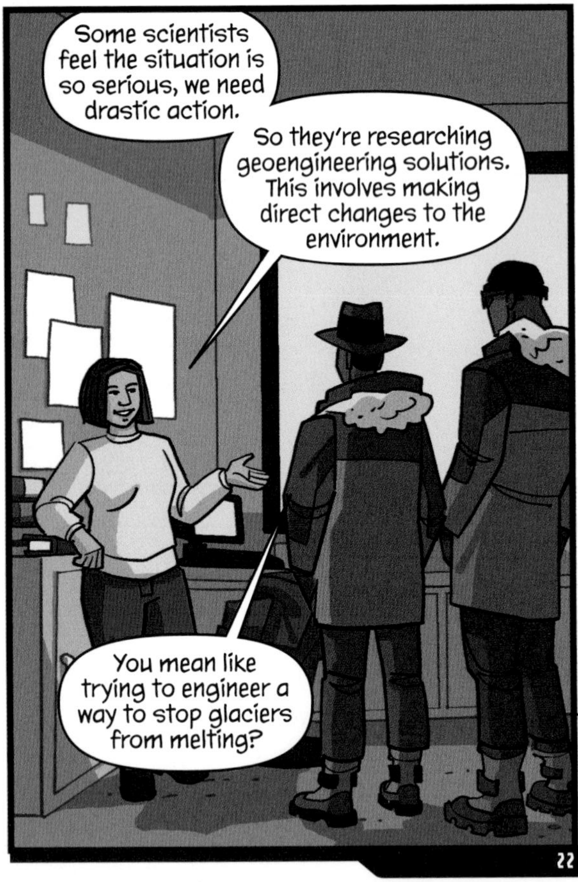
Some scientists feel the situation is so serious, we need drastic action.
So they're researching geoengineering solutions. This involves making direct changes to the environment.
You mean like trying to engineer a way to stop glaciers from melting?

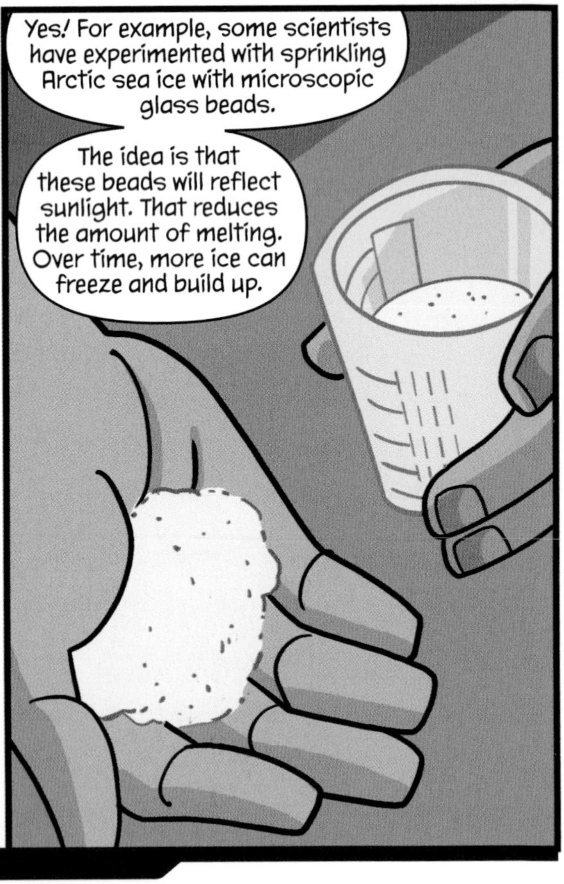
Yes! For example, some scientists have experimented with sprinkling Arctic sea ice with microscopic glass beads.
The idea is that these beads will reflect sunlight. That reduces the amount of melting. Over time, more ice can freeze and build up.

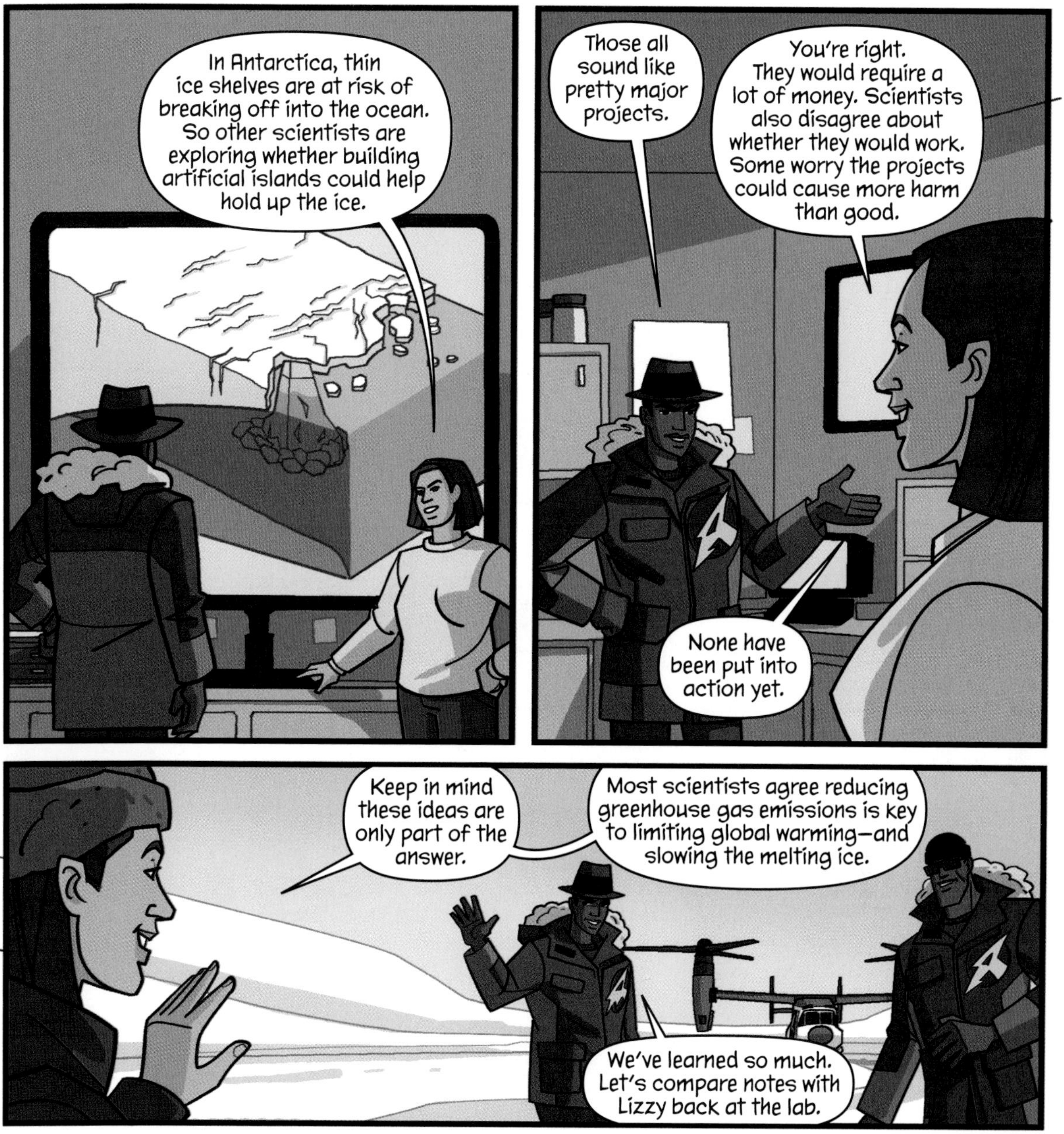
In Antarctica, thin ice shelves are at risk of breaking off into the ocean. So other scientists are exploring whether building artificial islands could help hold up the ice.
Those all sound like pretty major projects.
You're right. They would require a lot of money. Scientists also disagree about whether they would work. Some worry the projects could cause more harm than good.
None have been put into action yet.
Keep in mind these ideas are only part of the answer.
Most scientists agree reducing greenhouse gas emissions is key to limiting global warming—and slowing the melting ice.
We've learned so much. Let's compare notes with Lizzy back at the lab.

LIVING IN ANTARCTICA

Antarctica has 80 research stations run by teams of scientists from around the world. They study the climate, wildlife, astronomy, and geology. All together, an average of 5,000 people brave the harsh conditions, where temperatures can reach -128°F (-89°C)!

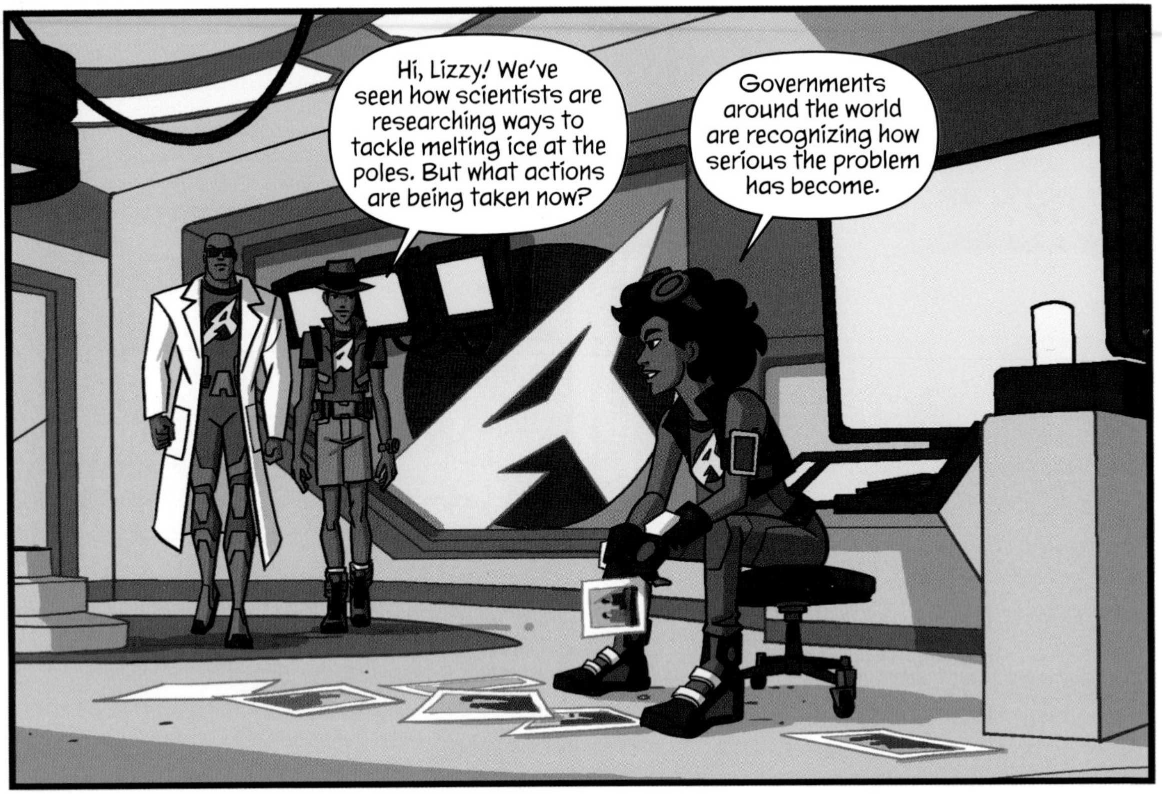
Hi, Lizzy! We've seen how scientists are researching ways to tackle melting ice at the poles. But what actions are being taken now?
Governments around the world are recognizing how serious the problem has become.

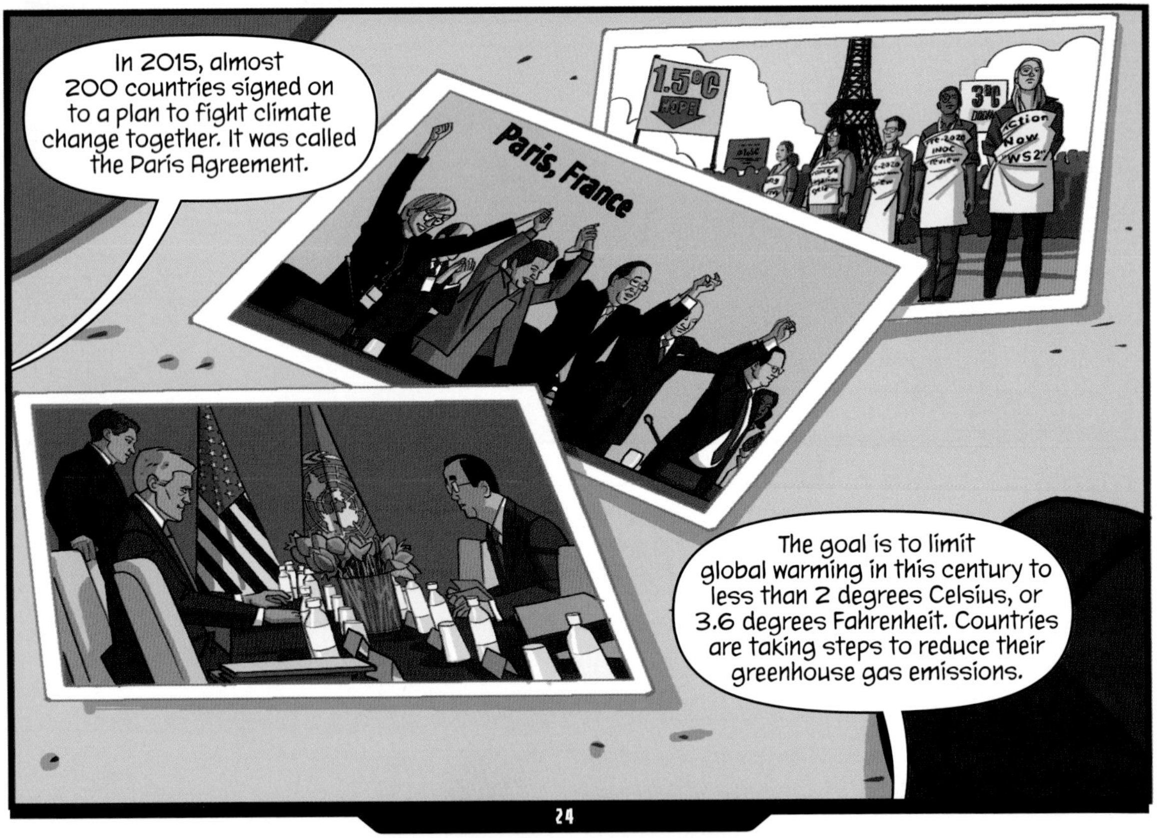
In 2015, almost 200 countries signed on to a plan to fight climate change together. It was called the Paris Agreement.
Paris, France
1.5°C
HOPE
The goal is to limit global warming in this century to less than 2 degrees Celsius, or 3.6 degrees Fahrenheit. Countries are taking steps to reduce their greenhouse gas emissions.

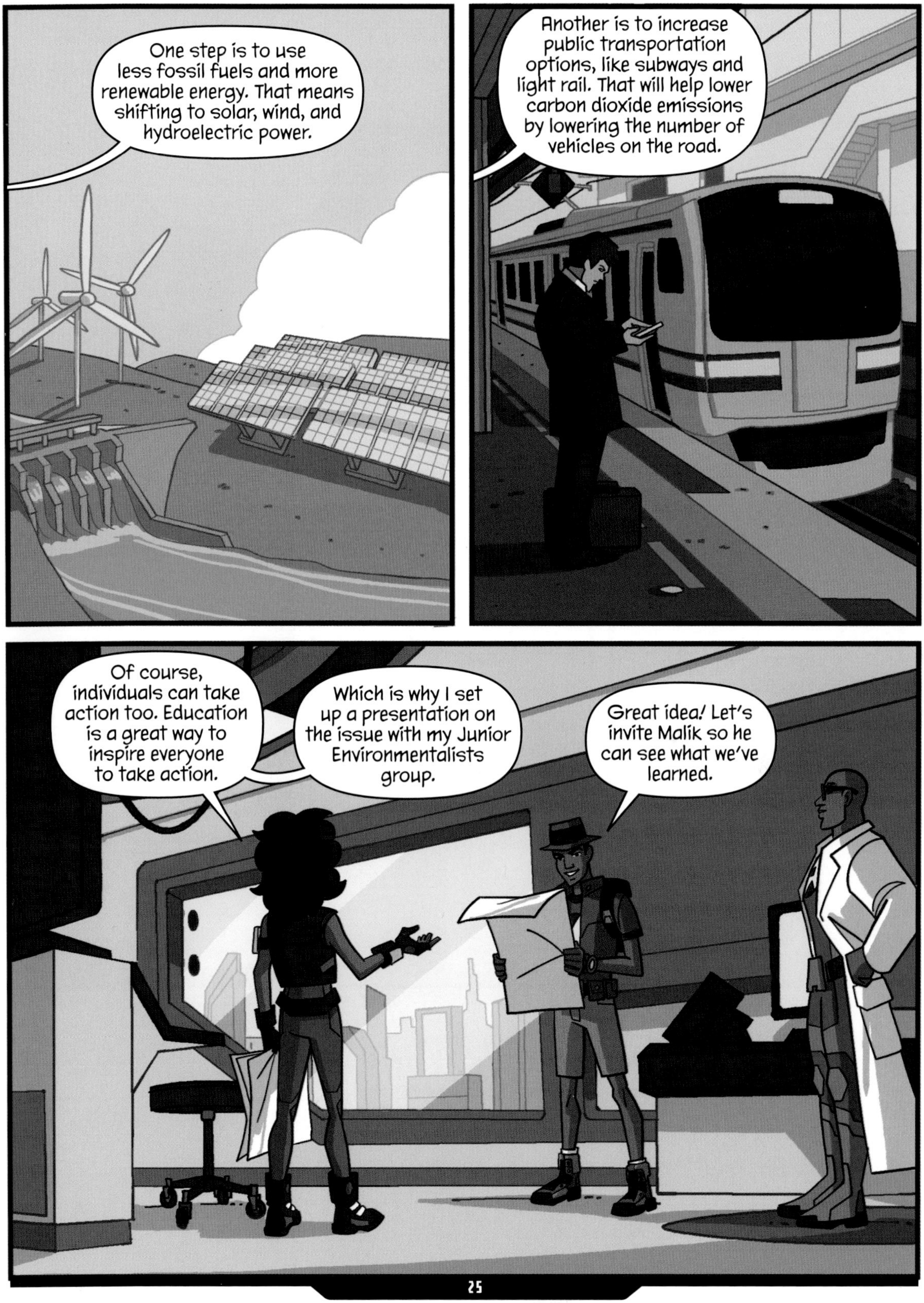
One step is to use less fossil fuels and more renewable energy. That means shifting to solar, wind, and hydroelectric power.
Another is to increase public transportation options, like subways and light rail. That will help lower carbon dioxide emissions by lowering the number of vehicles on the road.
Of course, individuals can take action too. Education is a great way to inspire everyone to take action.
Which is why I set up a presentation on the issue with my Junior Environmentalists group.
Great idea! Let's invite Malik so he can see what we've learned.

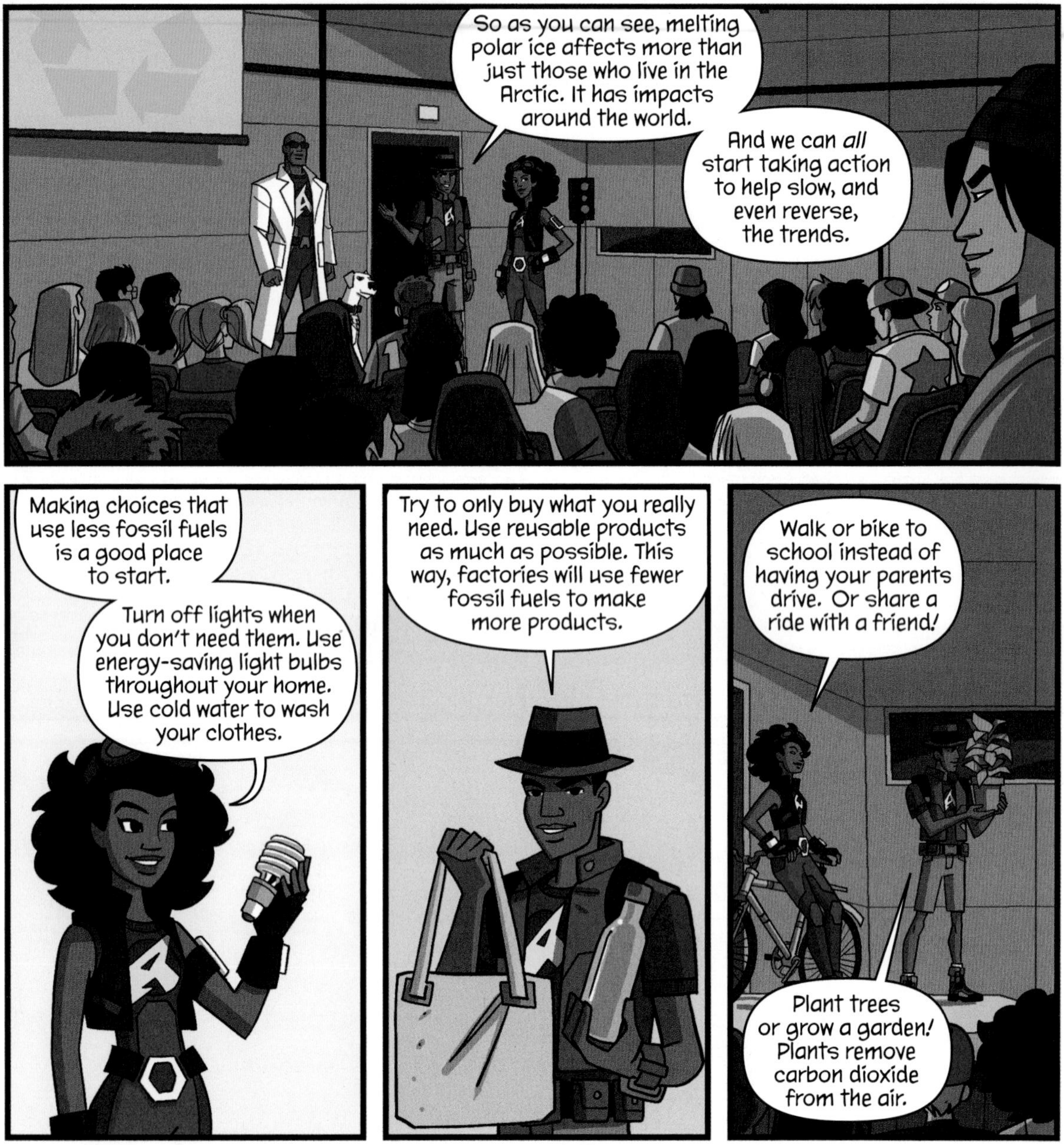
So as you can see, melting polar ice affects more than just those who live in the Arctic. It has impacts around the world.
And we can *all* start taking action to help slow, and even reverse, the trends.
Making choices that use less fossil fuels is a good place to start.
Turn off lights when you don't need them. Use energy-saving light bulbs throughout your home. Use cold water to wash your clothes.
Try to only buy what you really need. Use reusable products as much as possible. This way, factories will use fewer fossil fuels to make more products.
Walk or bike to school instead of having your parents drive. Or share a ride with a friend!
Plant trees or grow a garden! Plants remove carbon dioxide from the air.

CARBON FOOTPRINT CALCULATOR

A carbon footprint calculator estimates the amount of greenhouse gases your household creates through your actions. The average carbon footprint for a person in the U.S. is around 16 tons. Can you lower yours? See the Internet Sites section for a link to an online calculator.

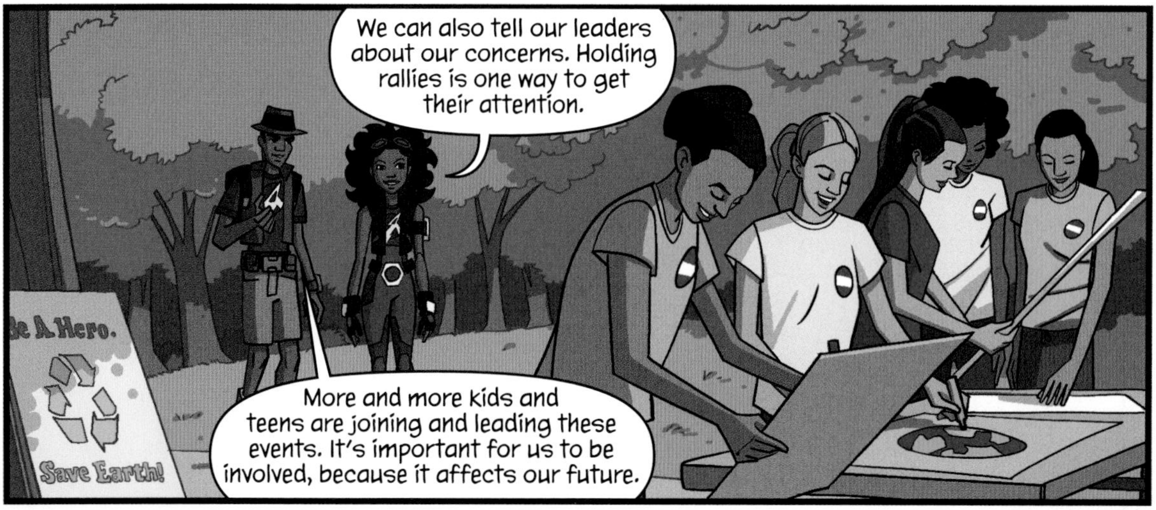
We can also tell our leaders about our concerns. Holding rallies is one way to get their attention.
More and more kids and teens are joining and leading these events. It's important for us to be involved, because it affects our future.
Save Earth!

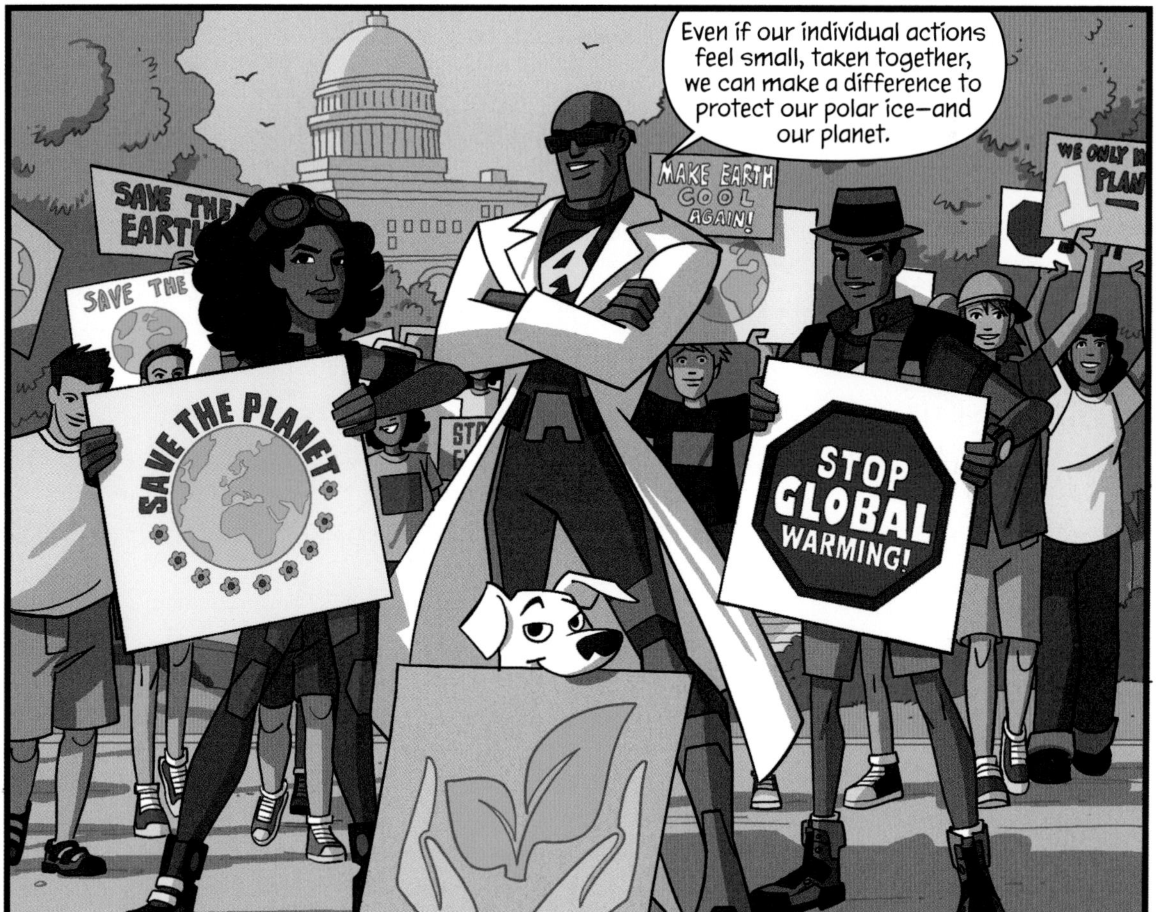
Even if our individual actions feel small, taken together, we can make a difference to protect our polar ice—and our planet.
MAKE EARTH COOL AGAIN!
SAVE THE PLANET
STOP GLOBAL WARMING!

TOTAL MELTDOWN

Global sea levels began rising in the early 1900s as polar ice started to melt. Records show a total rise in sea level of 5 to 8 inches (13 to 20 cm) since 1900.

BUT WHAT WOULD HAPPEN IF ALL THE ICE ON EARTH SUDDENLY MELTED?

- If all the ice on the entire planet melted, scientists estimate the sea level would rise 216 feet (66 m).

- Millions of people would be affected. A big part of the world's population lives in coastal areas. In the U.S., almost 40 percent of people have homes near the ocean.

- Eight of the world's ten largest cities are near the coast. If all the ice melted, U.S. cities such as New York, Boston, and San Francisco would be underwater. So would the entire state of Florida and the Eastern seaboard.

- Other cities across the globe would also be wiped out: London, Stockholm, Dublin, Venice, Tokyo, and Shanghai, just to name a handful.

- In South America, the Amazon basin and Paraguay river basin would become huge inlets of water. Cities such as Buenos Aires and Sao Paulo would be underwater.

- In Australia, the surge of water would create a massive inland sea in the southern part of the continent.

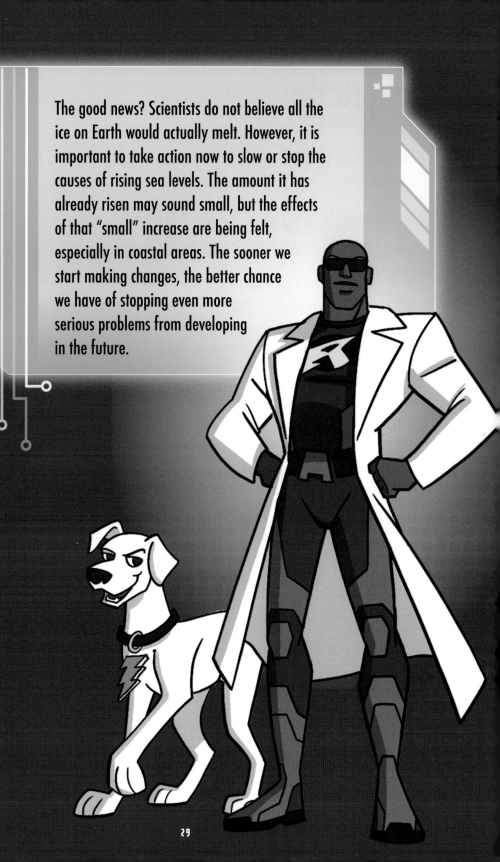

The good news? Scientists do not believe all the ice on Earth would actually melt. However, it is important to take action now to slow or stop the causes of rising sea levels. The amount it has already risen may sound small, but the effects of that "small" increase are being felt, especially in coastal areas. The sooner we start making changes, the better chance we have of stopping even more serious problems from developing in the future.

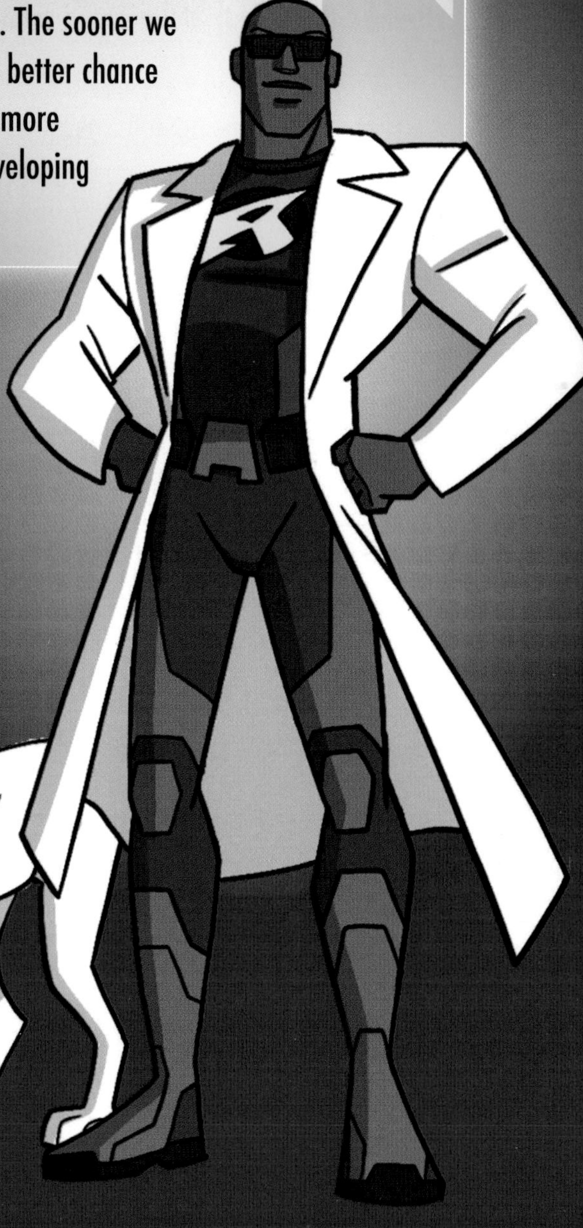

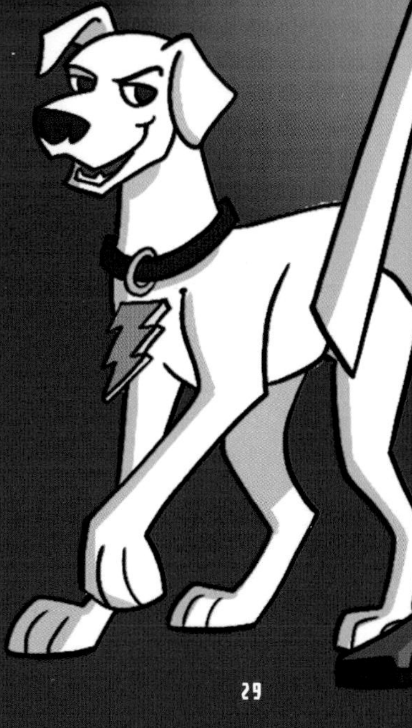

GLOSSARY

albedo effect (al-BEE-do ih-FEKT)—the ability of light surfaces to reflect more solar energy than dark surfaces

atmosphere (AT-muh-sfeer)—the mixture of gases that surrounds a planet

climate (KLY-muht)—the average weather of a place over a long period of time

emissions (ee-MIH-shunz)—substances discharged into the air

fossil fuel (FAH-suhl FYOOL)—a fuel formed in the Earth from the remains of plants and animals; coal, oil, and natural gas are fossil fuels

glacier (GLAY-shur)—a slow-moving mass of ice formed when snow falls and does not melt because temperatures remain below freezing

geoengineering (jee-oh-en-juh-NEER-ing)—designing and building things that have a direct impact on the environment and Earth's natural climate systems

greenhouse gas (GREEN-hows GAS)—a gas, such as carbon dioxide or methane, in Earth's atmosphere that traps heat energy from the sun

ice sheet (EYESS SHEET)—thick glacial ice that covers a large amount of land

iceberg (EYESS-burg)—a large mass of ice that has broken off from a glacier and floats in the sea

permafrost (PUR-muh-frawst)—a layer of ground that stays frozen

sea ice (SEE EYESS)—frozen seawater that floats on the ocean surface

READ MORE

Hand, Carol. *Melting Arctic Ice.* Minneapolis: Essential Library, an imprint of Abdo Publishing, 2018.

Herman, Gail. Illustrated by John Hinderliter. *What Is Climate Change?* New York: Penguin Workshop, an imprint of Penguin Random House, 2018.

Raij, Emily. *Climate Change and You: How Climate Affects Your Life.* North Mankato, MN: Capstone, 2020.

INTERNET SITES

CoolClimate Network: Carbon Footprint Calculator
coolclimate.berkeley.edu/calculator

NASA Climate Kids: What Is Climate Change?
climatekids.nasa.gov/climate-change-meaning/

The National Snow and Ice Data Center
nsidc.org/

INDEX